More Than Just a Braider
An Autobiographical Account

VOLUME I

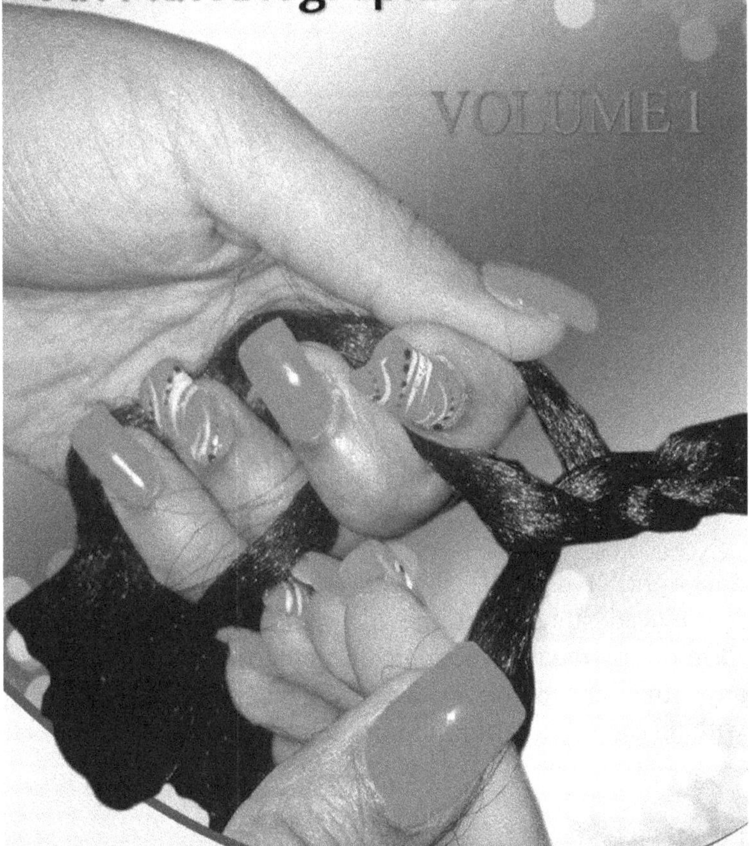

These Hands

This book is a work of non-fiction and is based solely upon the author's memory of the included events that have shaped her existence. To protect identities, names have been changed of all individuals, including that of the author.

CLF Publishing, LLC.
www.clfpublishing.org

Copyright © 2020 by These Hands.

All rights reserved. No portion of this book may be reproduced, stored in a retrieval system, or transmitted by any form or any means electronically, photocopied, recorded, or any other except for brief quotations in printed reviews, without the prior permission of the publisher.

ISBN # 978-1-945102-50-9

Cover Design by Senir Design. Contact information- info@senirdesign.com.

Printed in the United States of America.

DEDICATIONS

Grandma: I thank you for taking care of me beyond your eleven children. You always made home available to me throughout my childhood to the time I was an adult. I always had somewhere to lay my head no matter the time of day or night. I appreciate you for allowing me to see you go to work every day, to take care of home. I thank you for allowing me to return the favor of love, care, and appreciation while you were here.

Mom: This book is dedicated to you. I know for sure I could not have walked in your shoes. I kneel down and thank you, my queen. No, my childhood was nowhere near what's considered normal, but I am thankful. I thank you for all the knowledge and encouragement you gave. Yes, I got upset as a kid, but I quickly grew to understand. For as long as I have breath, I will always have your back. No, you did not raise me on a daily basis, but you have given me the gift of braiding and your words of encouragement to carry me along the way, and for that, I cherish and truly adore you until beyond the death of me.

ACKNOWLEDGEMENTS

For many years, I attempted to take the leap of faith to get this book done, but the fear of revisiting negative events and emotions caused me to procrastinate, so I would like to acknowledge Dr. C. White-Elliott, my publisher. She didn't help me take a leap; she straight out pushed me, and Dr. C, I thank you for it.

I would like to acknowledge all my clients, from the loyal and consistent to those who come occasionally, both in California and out of state. You *all* are appreciated. You are not just clients, but you grow to be family, and I appreciate you deeply.
You have encouraged me along the way and never gave up on me or my goals.

TABLE OF CONTENTS

Chapter One 7
Claire's Daughter

Chapter Two 14
Miss Pissy

Chapter Three 30
A Hard Head Makes a Soft Ass

Chapter Four 49
Oh, Baby!

Chapter Five 63
From Sin Town to Sin City

Chapter Six 75
'Til Death Do Us Part

Chapter Seven 87
What in the Law?

Chapter Eight 105
Out of Sight, Out of Mind

CHAPTER ONE
Claire's Daughter

All families experience some type of drama at one time or another. However, some families experience drama more often than others. Later though, that same drama can be laughed at over Thanksgiving and Christmas dinners years down the road. In other cases, thoughts of the drama will always bring tears, feelings of pain and/or regret, or sadness. Claire's experience falls in the category of the latter.

From 1971-74, when Claire was only fourteen through seventeen years old, a time of her life when she was experiencing the joys and pains of transitioning from puberty into womanhood, she experienced a life-altering situation that would change her life forever. Unbeknownst to her entire family, her mother's husband, the man she knew as Suga Daddy, began raping her when Claire's mother was away from the home. After the first occurrence, Claire told her mother in hopes her mother would do something to prevent the travesty from occurring again. However, to Claire's surprise and disappointment, her mother did not believe Claire's accusation. Claire, having nowhere to go and no one she could turn to, continued to reside in the home. Her lack of shelter elsewhere was the perfect situation for Suga Daddy, as that gave him continued access to her.

So, unfortunately, the rapes continued. On one specific occasion, while Claire was in the act of being sexually assaulted, her older sister walked into the room and witnessed their stepfather on top of Claire. Horrified, she grabbed an icepick and commenced to stabbing Suga Daddy, commanding that he immediately cease the cruel act he was committing upon her sister. Feeling the sharp, excruciating pains that infiltrated his body, Suga Daddy moved away from Claire in horror, seeking shelter from his attacker.

The wounds Suga Daddy received at the hands of his victim's sister sent him to the emergency room. When Claire's mother learned of what her husband had done and why he was in the hospital, she still did nothing to protect her daughter from being sexually abused. But, at that point, she did not need to intervene and protect Claire because although Suga Daddy remained in the home, with Claire and the rest of the family, he refrained from touching her.

Years later, when Claire was in her late twenties or early thirties, she began to date a young man named Matthew. Together, Matthew and Claire desired to build a life together. At the time, Claire was still living at home with her mother and stepfather. Eventually though, Claire and Matthew moved from their respective residences and rented an apartment together. Matthew took care of the majority of the financial responsibilities by working a job and selling drugs on the side. Claire, on the other hand, braided hair (which she had done for many years) to provide her own income. A few months later, Claire became pregnant and eventually gave birth to a daughter. Life progressed while Matthew worked and continued his hustle and Claire took care of the baby.

A typical day in Claire's life consisted of braiding hair- one client after the other- and taking care of her beautiful daughter. But, one fateful day in March of 1980 would prove to be drastically different. It would be a day no one would forget for the rest of their life.

Matthew was out making his drug rounds, driving through the streets of Pomona with a broken taillight. That was all that was needed to capture the attention of a local police officer. Behind Matthew's car, the lights on the police car flashed, and the siren sounded. In a panic, he pulled over but was fearful of being arrested for drug possession with the intent to sell. With haste, he swallowed the drugs (PCP), attempting to conceal them from the officers.

Matthew's plan did not go as anticipated. Yes, he avoided being arrested for drug possession, but what transpired afterward was not something Matthew could have ever predicted. Swallowing the drugs caused his blood stream to be flooded with deadly toxins. Slowly, Matthew became intoxicated by the drug. Not long after, he reached the home he shared with Claire and their daughter, relieved that the traffic stop did not turn out worse and that he had not been arrested.

When he entered the home, he greeted Claire in his normal manner and went along with business as usual. Slowly, his temperament changed, and Claire noticed how he began to act and speak in a strange manner. She had never witnessed such behavior from Matthew before. Out of nowhere, he began to mistake Claire for a demon or a monster. In his state of paranoia, he began attacking her. Claire had no choice but to defend herself against the threat of a wild man. To ward off his attacks, she picked up an ashtray and hit him with it. Instead of continuing to attack Claire, Matthew turned his attention to their three-month old daughter who was sitting in her car seat, which was positioned on the couch.

Looking down at his daughter, who he thought was another monster or demon, he pulled her from her car seat and began swinging her around, shaking her, and choking her. Claire screamed and screamed and screamed. Nothing she did or said could stop Matthew's erratic behavior. Before Claire could stop Matthew, he opened the front door of their apartment and had begun to descend the stairs with their daughter in his hands. As he ran down the stairs, he continued assaulting the baby by hitting her small, fragile body against the stairs' railings, causing further harm to her head, torso, and overall body. Unfortunately, that was not the extent of her injuries. Her father also dropped her to the ground, causing her to hit her head. He was treating her as though she was nothing more than a rag doll.

In the midst of the commotion, a good Samaritan was riding by on a motorcycle. Hearing strange noises, the motorcyclist looked over at Matthew to see what the strange sounds were that he was hearing. The motorcyclist witnessed the devastation that was occurring right before his eyes. To bring an end to the dreadful and deadly series of events, the motorcyclist ran his bike directly into Matthew, attempting to cause an immediate cease to his actions and to save the baby who was obviously in harm's way. After being hit with the bike twice, Matthew dropped his daughter and ran away, seemingly to protect himself from harm. Others eventually heard the commotion and ran outside, but any efforts of assistance they may have attempted to render were futile. The baby girl was severely injured, and her injuries immediately caused her earthly demise.

Sometime later, the coroner, the police, and the paramedics showed up, but Matthew was not present at the scene. Consequently, the police were required to detect his location. When he was discovered, he was completely nude and attempting to hide out in a section of rose bushes on the campus of a nearby junior high school. Noticing Matthew's erratic behavior, the police officers took him into custody but decided he required medical attention. So, paramedics placed Matthew inside an ambulance and whisked him away to the hospital. With the criminal element embedded in Matthew's situation, police cars followed the ambulance to the hospital, as he legally remained in their custody. At the hospital, it was learned that Matthew had consumed PCP, and the drugs had made him hallucinate, which led to the incident with his family.

Days later, after the drugs were cleared from Matthew's system, he was remanded into the custody of the State of California. Charges were brought against Matthew, and a trial was scheduled. At the end of the trial, Matthew was convicted of second-degree murder (non-premeditated murder/manslaughter) and sentenced to seven years within a state prison of which he served the full term.

Not long after Matthew was sent to prison, Claire began counseling to help her deal with the grief of losing both her three-month old daughter to death and her long-time boyfriend to prison. The entire string of events had occurred suddenly and were unfathomable. The events caused Claire to go into a tailspin, feeling very lost and confused and without comfort. Unfortunately, counseling alone was not enough to ease Claire's woes, so her psychiatrist prescribed psychotropic medication to assist in Claire's recovery of her mental and emotional state. As time drew on, Claire continued to experience severe depression and eventually turned to street drugs to self-medicate, hoping she could lose herself and her pain in the euphoria created by drug inducement.

Then, on a quiet and seemingly normal day, Claire encountered Jacob, an old friend with whom she had gone to high school. Their chance meeting led to a one-night stand. The one-night stand was the extent of their "relationship." Jacob was already in a long-term relationship with a woman named Shonna, and they already had a child together, so he was not looking for anything permanent with Claire. During that same time frame, Claire was continuing counseling and had even forgiven Matthew for his actions that had led to their daughter's death. Their relationship flourished, and they were married while Matthew was still incarcerated. Because of the marriage, Claire and Matthew were permitted conjugal visits.

Not much later, Claire learned that either the visits with her new husband or her fling with Jacob had led to her second pregnancy. Claire was unsure which man had fathered her unborn child, but she told her husband the unborn baby was his, hoping her words were true. Time, however, would not fail to reveal the truth. When the time came to deliver, Claire gave birth to a healthy beautiful baby daughter.

I am that daughter. I am Phoebe.
Claire is my mother.
The baby girl who died much too early was the big sister I never had the pleasure to meet. It was her death that eventually led to my life coming to be.
If Matthew had not gone to prison, Claire would have probably never had a fling with Jacob, and I would have never been born. You see, Jacob is my father, not Matthew.

And, this is my story.

CHAPTER TWO
Miss Pissy

In February of 1981, on a semi-cool day, I, Phoebe, was born in the city of Pomona, in Southern California. At the time of my birth, my mother was living with my maternal grandmother and her stepfather, Suga Daddy. She had moved from the apartment she had shared with her boyfriend Matthew, as she could not bear residing in the place her daughter had lost her life. My mother was still suffering greatly from her loss, and one may have thought she would be happy to have another baby in her life, but that was not quite the case.

I cannot tell you from my own memory what transpired directly after my birth; however, I was told my mother would not hold me, caress me, or cuddle with me when I was born because she imagined bruises and scars being on my body as they had been on my older sister on the day she died. And, maybe she thought getting too close to me would cause a bond to be created and maybe she feared having me ripped from her life as my older sister had been. For her, that would have been unbearable. So, she refrained from having close interaction with me. All my cuddling and nurturing was left to other family members, such as my aunts who visited from time to time from

New Orleans, my aunts who live here in California, my uncles, and my grandmother who was my primary caregiver.

My first memory of myself is at age four. During that time, I would often be surrounded by my uncles, who would be involved in different activities. I recall watching one of them riding his beach cruiser nearly every day. It always appeared as though he was having loads of fun. So, one day, without permission, I decided it was my turn to have a little fun. So, I grabbed the beach cruiser (with no prior experience with riding a bike at all), and I climbed aboard. Off I went down the street, riding the bicycle while standing. If I had attempted to sit on the seat of the bike, I would not have been able to reach the pedals. Remember, I was only four years old, so I was rather short. When I reached the end of the block, I carefully and slowly turned the bike around and made my way back towards our house.

When I returned from my joyride, I was confronted by a host of family members who stood on the sidewalk awaiting my return. Amongst them was my uncle, the owner of the bike, who along with another uncle were proctors at high schools. Both loved to skate, and one loved to box in his spare time. Both were very active in the neighborhood and were well-known and respected.

As I approached the crowd of family, they applauded my success at riding the large bike, but they also scolded me for my disobedience in the same breath. My uncle grabbed me, so he could stop the bike. I had no idea how to do that. I was just riding! Even with the chastisement, the ride was worth every moment of exhilaration I experienced. And, if given the chance, I would have done it again in a heartbeat.

Living in the home with my grandparents and me were two of my maternal cousins, one male and one female, who were siblings. Their mother resided in New Orleans. Officially, my mother lived in our home as well, but she was in and out of prison on a regular basis, so I did not really consider her living with us. When she was home, she would busy herself with cleaning, as she listened to music and sang along. She has a beautiful voice, and her melodies warmed my heart. After cleaning the interior of our home, she and her broom would move outdoors, where she swept the porch, the walkways, and the sidewalk in front of the house. She is the only one I know who does that.

Then, as time went on, it was not a matter of 'if' she would return to jail or prison; it was a matter of 'when.' Her continued stints of incarceration stemmed from missing her probation appointments due to her addiction to psych meds and her use of street drugs.

Unfortunately, my mother's drug addiction led to her taking my belongings, selling them to feed her habit. However, her addiction affected me in other ways as well. For example, she would often take me with her to her clients' homes when she had braiding appointments. I enjoyed going with her, but I did not enjoy how those visits ended. Most times, we would walk to their homes because my mother did not own a car. Along the walks, she would teach me life lessons, telling me to be strong, not to turn out like her, and to stand on my own feet. She would also tell me how beautiful I am and so on.

Once we arrived to her client's home, she would commence her 'job.' While she braided, I watched how her fingers would maneuver the hair. I was entranced by her skills and a desire to braid grew inside of me. So, I would practice on my own hair, taking small sections and allowing my fingers to move methodically as I had seen hers do. To me, her fingers looked as though they were plucking the strings of a harp.

Those times together with my mother were very memorable. But, they would not always end so well. As soon as my mother had completed the hairstyle and was paid, she would immediately go into her disappearing act. She would tell the woman whose hair she had just braided that she was going outside to smoke or that she needed to run to the store. She would leave on her supposed brief journey, which was never brief at all. Once she left, she never returned, leaving me in the company of strangers. My grandmother would be contacted, basically forcing her to come and retrieve me from the stranger's home. Because my grandmother did not drive, at times, she had to ride the bus or walk to pick me up.

Other times, my grandmother sent my uncle to retrieve me. Again, that was my reality. Although my mother loved me, her full attention was on covering up her pain. Her pain relief was drugs because they kept her intoxicated, oblivious to the pain that lurked inside her heart and mind, consuming her. After I returned home from the client's home, I would not see my mother again until late that same night or some time the next day.

On days when life was calm, my cousins and I would entertain ourselves by jumping Double Dutch and singing in out trio, moving around the living room with a brush that was our pretend microphone. Other times, we would pull out an old mattress and use it to flip on. Being kids, we did what we thought was fun and what made us happy.

Then one day, seemingly out of nowhere, my grandmother went on a rampage. All I heard was yelling and screaming. Before I knew it, the door opened, and my fourteen-year-old female cousin went running down the street as she screamed a blood-curdling scream. My grandmother was not far behind her, swinging the tree branch she had been using to beat my cousin. Later, I learned my grandmother's tirade began because she had learned my cousin was pregnant. My grandmother only wanted the best for all of us, and when my cousin ended up pregnant -at fourteen- my grandma was disappointed. Nevertheless, after some time, life returned to normal for my female cousin. Grandmother had calmed down, and my cousin delivered a healthy girl, whom my cousin named

Diamond. She was so light that she looked white, with her greenish/blue eyes.

Not too long after the incident of my cousin getting beat with a tree branch (before her baby was born), the normal life that I was accustomed to experiencing on a daily basis for the first four years of my life was disrupted in one of the most horrific ways when I was five years old.

One night, I was asleep on the living room couch as usual. As I lay asleep on my stomach, I awoke, feeling the sensation of needed to have a bowel movement. My only thought was rising up to go to the restroom. When I lifted my head to begin my ascent from the couch, the back of my head hit something. Quickly, I turned my head. To my surprise, my male cousin was lying on top of me with his penis in my rectum. He asked, "Does it hurt?" I nodded yes. He pulled out from me, and I proceeded with making my way to the bathroom.

He stood there watching me, warning me not to tell of his sadistic behavior. If I did, he threatened I would get the same type of beating from our grandmother that his sister had received not long before. His threat scared me to my core. I definitely did not want to be beat- in any manner- so, I kept my mouth closed. After his threat, he commenced to urinating, making me watch him. As I watched, he asked me if I liked looking at him and if I wanted to touch him. I said no to both questions.

After that horrifying incident, I had to devise a plan that would keep him away from me. The first part of the plan was to stay awake throughout the night, so I could be aware of what was occurring. I did this by watching television. The second part of the plan was to wet my bed (the couch) to keep him away from me. I figured no one would want to touch a wet, smelly girl. I was correct in my thinking because on one occasion my cousin did attempt to violate me again, but when he felt I was wet, he moved away. There were two downsides of my plan. *First,* a nickname resulted from my wetting the bed. My cousin began calling Miss Pissy, and everyone else followed suit. He thought teasing me would make me stop wetting the bed, so he could resume his activity. However, his plan did not work. I continued wetting the bed.

Second, my grandmother became aware of me keeping the television on, so she would come in at night and turn it off. These two methods were successful in keeping my cousin away from me at night, but it did not stop him from making me watch him urinate or asking me to touch him, which I never did. My grandmother learned of my bedwetting, and all she said was, "Keep the couch clean." Following her instructions, I would take a washcloth and place a little detergent and bleach on it to scrub the cushion I had soiled with urine. Then, I would place the cushion in the sunlight to allow it to dry.

As part of my everyday home life, we raised chickens. We kept them in our backyard, and when they became nice and plump, they would become a great feast. One day, I was in the backyard with my mother, and I took a slice of bread to feed the chickens. The chickens took the bread and tried to take me along as part of their meal. They attacked me from my forehead to my pinky toe. To this date, I have a permanent scar on my forehead from the brutal attack.

Soon after the 'chicken attack', it was time for me to begin my formal education in kindergarten in an institution of learning. Because my grandmother worked, she would be unavailable each day to walk me to school or pick me up afterward. It was required of me to fend for myself. But before my grandmother left me on my own, she walked me to school and told me our trip together was going to occur that one day and that one day only. From there, I would be required to remember the directions, so I could get to school and back home on my own. The sound of her request was scary, but I was determined to meet her demands.

As we walked to the meet and greet, where parents and students would meet teachers, Grandmother gave me a long lecture about keeping my mouth closed and not telling the "white folks" at my school our family business. I thought her request was bizarre, but I knew she was serious, so I obeyed. I later learned that my grandmother did not care much for white people because of the privilege they carried compared to blacks. Her personal knowledge of them came when she was required to drop out of junior high to work. She worked cleaning the homes of whites who would degrade and belittle her as she cleaned. That experience left a bad taste in her mouth and bad thoughts in her psyche.

As the days went on, I began walking to school, staying to myself and keeping my mouth closed. Along the way, I would see other children, but I did not say anything to them. They were a bit friendlier than I was. They would try to talk to me, but at first, I would not respond. Finally, they asked me what school I was walking to. I told them, and they said they were going to the same school. We began walking together every morning. After school, we would go to our "meet up" spot, so we could walk home together. That made getting home much easier and much more fun.

One day, while walking home from school, my friends and I witnessed a white guy, who was dressed in a mechanic's uniform, jump the fence into the wash that was near our house. We could not believe what we were seeing, so we ran to the fence for a closer look. Some of the kids said he must have been on dope. I suggested he must have been depressed or both. The kids thought my suggestion was weird. Then, feelings of disgust grew, as we saw the trail of blood moving through the shallow water. Apparently, the blood had come from the back of the man's head. I was in somewhat of a trance, as I tried to visualize the damage he sustained when he had fallen.

Shortly afterward, we heard sirens, as the fire department came to the scene. Seeing us, they made us clear out. When I arrived home, I shared the incident with my grandmother. She said sometimes she feels like jumping into the wash herself. When I asked her why, she told me I was too young to understand.

After school, I had to feed myself because on most days, no one would be home. I would prepare cheese toast from the block of government cheese that we stood in a long line for once a month. I also made sugar toast, syrup and peanut butter sandwiches (which were my favorite), and noodles. We also had cereal, but I did not eat that because we had roaches and plus, I did not like powered milk. We kept the bread safe in the refrigerator, so I was the sandwich and noodle queen.

On other days, to my disappointment though, when I would arrive home, my male cousin would be there. My grandmother and uncle would be at work, and my female cousin would be out somewhere. Constantly, he would ask me to watch him urinate and inquire about whether I wanted to touch him or not. I would walk away, going to sit at the kitchen table to complete my homework. The warnings to not tell continued as well.

Even with incidents such as the one with my male cousin, life was not always strange. My grandmother worked hard to make life 'normal' for me. On my sixth birthday, to my surprise, my grandmother bought me a bike of my own. I was ecstatic. I rode it the entire day, completely ignoring my other gifts. The next day, to my dismay, the bike was gone. I found out later that my mother had stolen it, so she could sell it to obtain drug money. After that birthday, my mother stealing and selling my presents was the norm, and I came to expect it. It was very disheartening, but it was my reality.

Then, when one would think life couldn't get any more interesting or twisted for me, it did. On the way home one day when I was six or seven years old, the regular group of kids I walked home with was walking together. Two of them, who were cousins, told me they knew my mother and that she often goes to their house. When I saw my mom, I told her what the kids had told me. So, she started taking me to their home for visits with her. One day, when we were there, after playing for a while, I went looking for my mother. I couldn't find her anywhere. Seeing me looking frantically, one of the kids said, "Look in the garage."

I entered the garage door, and I saw my mother holding a crack pipe, inhaling the smoke from the melting cocaine, while a man and woman looked on. When she saw me, she dropped the pipe and yelled, "Go in the house!" Dropping the pipe caused the man to get upset. I ran out of there quickly. A little later, I began to play in the backyard with the other children, as if though nothing had transpired. Then, we heard yelling, and we went running toward the voices. In the kitchen, my mother was holding a knife to her chest, and I could see a spot of blood where the knife had punctured her skin. She was crying and saying she had nothing for which to live. The man tried to encourage her, telling her we all loved her.

I felt a pain grab my chest. Her words made me feel as though I did not matter, and although my heart hurt, I spoke out anyway. I yelled, "Mom, I'm right here!" My words were meant to encourage her and let her know she was not alone. Finally, the man was able to wrestle the knife from my mother's hands, but not without getting himself cut a bit here and there in the process. After calming my mother down, the man told her to go lie down in the back bedroom. That was the first time I remember crying. Seeing my mother hurting, hurt me.

We both ended up spending the night there. I slept on the living room couch. The next morning, I awoke to my mother gently rubbing my face and my hair. When she saw my eyes open, she explained she was not herself the night before, and she apologized for the words she had spoken. She said she always had a lot on her mind and sometimes it got the best of her, making her tired of everything. Those feelings drained her, causing her to not want to live. She ended the conversation by reassuring me that she loved me.

At seven years old, I was walking with my mother through the neighborhood. We were on our way home from the fish market. My mother was giving me her pearls of wisdom in between bites of fish. All of a sudden, a van pulled up next to us, and several parole officers jumped out. Because my mother had once again violated parole, one of the officers promptly took her plate from her hand and another one put handcuffs on her, placing her under arrest. Another officer took my hand and proceeded to walk me down the street towards home. My grandmother, hearing of the incident from passerby's, began to walk to our location. She took me from the officer and walked me home. Seeing my mother loaded into the van hurt my heart, and tears fell from my eyes. That is the second time I remember crying.

Although I was accustomed to my mother being in and out of my life and not seeing her on a daily basis, I was not prepared for her to be away for a solid year or two, which is what resulted after her arrest. During the time of her absence, my grandmother attempted to keep my life as 'normal' as possible. Our life consisted of her coming home from a twelve-hour long day, which included her working hours and the time she spent on the bus, to spend the evening with me. Once she arrived home, she would change into her moo-moo gowns and sit on the front porch to water her rose bushes. She was well-known throughout the neighborhood from the popularity of her children and her grandchildren (good or bad). Adults and children would either drive by or walk by and wave to her. Meanwhile, I would hang out with a neighbor's daughter, flipping on that dirty mattress, playing "That's My Car," hoola-hooping, Miss Mary Mack, and hopscotch until the street lights came on.

My grandmother also took the time to show me how to write my mother a letter. I did so once, only because I was upset with my mother for always leaving me, but I did not really want to write letters. After that, I never did so again. Despite my neglect of writing to my mother, she would write to me all the time, sending letters and cards. Instead of communicating with her in writing, I preferred to speak with her by telephone. She called often, and we kept in touch.

During my mother's absence, my grandmother kept me entertained and around family. One of my uncles, who was in the military, always comforted me when he was in town. When he came home, he would always have a gift for me. My favorite gift was a suede black Nike sweat suit that had my name on it. During his visits, my uncle would play oldies, hold me, and cry. His grief came from the loss of his daughter, who was killed in a car accident along with her mother and other siblings. The comfort he gave me came from missing her. Unfortunately, I never got a chance to meet her, but there was a large portrait of her over the fireplace, so I saw her every day.

Also, my grandmother permitted me to ride the Valley Connection to my cousin's house. However, she sent my male cousin along with me, so he could protect me from strangers, harm, and danger. Unbeknownst to my grandmother, my cousin was the one I required protection from. While on the Valley Connection, I looked forward to spending time with my girl cousin who was only slightly older than I was. Ruining my moment, my cousin exposed his penis to me and asked me to touch it. I told him I was going to tell the bus driver. My threat caused my cousin to quickly tuck himself away.

When I arrived to my girl cousin's home, I told my aunt what had transpired, and she immediately called my grandmother, who is her mother, and reported the incident. When I arrived home, my grandmother never said a word to me about it. At the same time though, I never had any further inappropriate interactions with my cousin. I assumed she had spoken with him about his behavior, thereby halting all inappropriate behavior. One month later, my male cousin was expelled from school because he had exposed himself to another student. After that incident, my grandmother sent him to New Orleans, back to his mother.

During that first visit to my cousin's home, I accompanied her to her tennis lesson. The coach always gave everyone their first lesson free. That day, I received a free lesson. The coach was so impressed with my skill level that he invited me to be on his team. I was excited. Later, when I told my grandmother about it, she said, "I'm not paying for that." So, I let it go. That night, when we returned to my cousin's home, my uncle began to pressure my cousin to be more interested in tennis and to try harder. In the process, he compared her to me, which only served to make her uncomfortable and was a seed planted to cause her to resent me. The truth is- she did not have any desire to play tennis, and her father's pressure did nothing to increase her interest.

On the second and last visit to my cousin's home, my uncle assisted my cousin with her homework while my aunt cooked dinner. My cousin was having a difficult time catching on to the concept. I, however, was able to answer the question my uncle had posed, as my cousin looked on. That infuriated my uncle who was paying for my cousin to go to private school. He made a comment about her going to private school and the fact that

I *only* went to public school. I didn't understand the difference in the two school systems, but I do remember feeling badly about his disposition toward me and public school. He really did not welcome me to their home, as he was concerned about me being a bad influence on his daughter. To make matters worse, my cousin told me she always got into trouble when I was there because I did more than she did and I knew more than she did, causing her to look bad. After that weekend, I never rode the bus over there again.

During that time frame, my grandfather Suga Daddy passed away. One day he was working on his truck, which was uplifted on a jack. Somehow, the truck came off the jack and rolled over him, killing him. That was all I was told about the incident.

Meanwhile, school for me was going well. The only problem I experienced was being called into the office often because my clothes constantly smelled of smoke. My grandmother smoked, and I informed the principal that was the only reason my clothes carried odors of cigarette smoke. In an effort to change my home situation as it related to my grandmother's nicotine habit, I would be sent home with pamphlets sharing the dangers of second-hand smoke.

CHAPTER THREE
A Hard Head Makes a Soft Ass

By the time I turned eight years old, I was preparing to move from the home I had lived in for the first seven years of my life. The aunt that I visited when riding the Valley Connection convinced my grandmother to sell her home and get an apartment in the same building that she and her family lived in. Our neighborhood was growing increasingly worse due to fights, drugs, gangs, more frequent drive-by's, and the traffic that was moving in and out of our house. To top it off, people were constantly running through our yard to go through the wash, trying to get away from the police. Obviously, my grandmother agreed with my aunt because we packed up, and off we went to a new neighborhood in Pomona.

For me, the new move required an adjustment period because many changes took place. For one, I enrolled into a new school. Two, I was in a new environment. Three, I had to become accustomed to city life and having interaction with more people in the apartment complex versus living on a street with houses. For my grandmother, things were visibly and physically better. She had retired from her job, which meant she no longer had to walk and ride the bus on a daily basis.

Furthermore, there were less people coming in and out of the house, such as uncles and miscellaneous people. At the same time though, she became more of a recluse, staying in her room when she was home. Her cooking schedule shifted as well. At that point, she only cooked on Sundays.

In our new home, it was just my grandmother and me. My uncles had moved on, and my female cousin, who was pregnant at fourteen years old, would only come with her daughter to visit from time to time. The only regular visits we had were from the family who lived in the same apartment complex: my aunt and cousin. For entertainment, my aunt would take us shopping and to eat from time to time. My aunt was very smart and great with math, counting money, and budgeting as we shopped. She was also very clean. She would require the waitresses to clean the table prior to us eating our meals. I loved watching her in action.

My grandmother loved fried chicken, so one of the places my aunt would take us was Pioneer Chicken. Since the move, we could no longer cook our own chicken from the backyard, so we would buy it from the grocery store or pick it from somewhere, such as Pioneer. My grandmother would always say, "It doesn't taste like home, but it will do." The Golden Ox was another place we would go when my aunt treated us to a day out. That was something I always looked forward to.

Other than making the aforementioned adjustments, life was pretty routine with the exception of visiting my physician on a few occasions. Compared to other girls my age, I was rather small in stature, appearing to be suffering from malnutrition. At times, I would stay in my room, lying in the sunlight to keep warm. This, of course, was concerning to my grandmother. When she took me to my physician, we learned I suffer from anemia. To increase my iron levels, my grandmother began to prepare liver for me to consume.

During the doctor visits, I became enthralled and mesmerized by the nurses, as I watched them perform their job with care and concern. From my experiences, a desire grew within me to enter the nursing profession, so I could care for others who suffer from various ailments.

During that time, my mother was released from prison. She would visit me for my birthdays, but the pattern she had demonstrated when I was younger had not halted. The next day, my gifts would always be stolen with the purpose of selling them to gain drug money. Although her behavior was hurtful, I came to expect it. Truthfully, I had grown out of being excited about gifts for birthdays and Christmas. I was just happy to have my mother near me.

Through all the different behaviors my mother exhibited, her mother continued trying to assist her. For example, my grandmother would give my mother bus fare, so she could go to her parole appointments. Instead of my mother using the funds as intended, she would purchase cigarettes for herself and Martinelli's apple juice for me. Did she attend her appointments? Most times she did. How did she get there if she spent the bus fare on cigarettes? She walked!

On one occasion, she took me with her. That particular appointment was all the way in Ontario, and we walked there from Pomona; she had her cigarettes and I had my apple juice. Along the way, she told me to always stand on my own. And even if I have a car, which is great, never be afraid to walk where I need to go, if that is what it takes. And, as usual, she encouraged me to always seek to better myself.

By that time, my mother had stopped braiding hair, but I had been practicing, so I could improve my skills. I would try different styles on my own hair, and my cousin, who had the baby, would always ask me to try one style or another on her. If I braided someone's hair, I did not charge because I was still learning. I had come to love braiding, as it was a time and space of meditation for me. It was a time I could escape thinking about anything going on in my life and only concern myself with perfecting my craft and making the style fit the person, while making the person look and feel good. That was always something I wanted for myself, but there is always a satisfying joy in transforming someone's outer appearance by braiding their hair, impacting their personal outlook of themselves.

In third grade, I was very active in school, playing soccer, tetherball, basketball with the boys, and on the monkey bars. My teacher suggested I take gymnastics and offered me a free lesson. I took the free lesson and impressed the coach, who in turn wanted me to stay and practice on a regular basis. I would have loved to, but when I asked my grandmother about it, she responded the same way she had when I expressed my desire to try tennis: "I'm not paying for that."

Later that year, my mother went to jail again. She was scheduled to visit her parole officer, so she took me along with her. While she was there, she was required to take a drug test via a urine sample. She did; however, the results came back "dirty." A requirement of her probation was to remain drug free. The "dirty" test demonstrated she had not complied with her probationary conditions, so she was arrested.

As all of that transpired, I sat in the lobby, waiting for my mother, so we could take the walk back home. Instead of seeing my mother, an officer approached me. He was coming to retrieve me, so he could drive me home. To say I was infuriated with the chain of events is an understatement. I was extremely angry that my mother was always spinning through the revolving door of my life. I asked my grandmother, "Why does Mom love drugs more than me?"

Not only did my mother's absence bother me, but my life in general was disconcerting. I began to look outside myself, and I realized life was different for me compared to the lives of other children. Their conversations consisted of home life with their parents and siblings. Not only were their conversations different, but when the time came to complete family tree assignments for school, the story my tree told was always different. Listening to their conversations and viewing their family trees led me to have a conversation of my own with my grandmother. When I inquired about my family and the absenteeism of my mother, my grandmother revealed to me the incident involving my mother and the death of her first child. That conversation led to her explaining how the trauma my mother suffered debilitates the control she has over her own mind and how the lack of control leads to a constant desire to escape to another place, hence, the causation of her drug abuse.

Meanwhile, life was progressing for everyone, everywhere. My male cousin, who had been sent to live in New Orleans, had signed a contract with an up-and-coming record label. He was doing well with his music. The family was excited and supportive of him. But then, something transpired, and he was shot at point-blank range in his chest- leading to his death. My grandmother told me about the incident after she got the phone call, but no one told us exactly what had occurred. Privately, I wondered if he had been caught touching someone's child.

During my fifth-grade year an event transpired that would eventually serve as a catalyst to the turn my life would one day take. One day, as I played on the playground, two young boys walked up to me and introduced themselves by telling me they were my brothers and that there were more siblings at their home. I did not know what to think when I heard their words. What I did know was someone had to have answers.

When I returned home, I questioned my grandmother, looking for answers. My grandmother informed me the two boys were not my brothers and that people would say they are related to me, but they are just friends of my mother. For some reason, I did not believe her due to her awkward body language, and I decided to run away. The next day after school, instead of going home, I went home with the two boys. There, I met their father, who told me he is my father too. I didn't know what to believe then, but I eventually found out their words were true.

The next day, I went to school as usual. Sometime during the course of the day, my grandmother showed up at the school and told me she knew where I had been the night before and to not let it happen again. She told me to be sure I went home after school and nowhere else. She said it so calmly yet sternly that I quickly got a visual of the branch she used to whip my cousin. Scared of what would happen if I disobeyed, I chose to follow her orders. From that point forward, I went straight home.

Later in fifth grade, I participated in a school production. In it, I sang "The Greatest Love of All." I was happy that day because my grandmother was there to see me in action. Because she smoked, walking long distances was difficult, so she refrained from tasking her body. As a result, she did not attend many school functions. Here is the perfect example: At the end of my fifth-grade year, I was promoted to the sixth grade. I walked across the stage and received my certificate. But, there was no one from my family there to witness it. No one. Not my grandmother. Not my mother. So, I walked home alone with my certificate in hand.

After the summer passed, and it was time to begin sixth grade, I began at a new school. I felt awkward because I did not fit in, and I was still skinny and underdeveloped. All the girls, from one group to the next, were focused on boys and being popular. At that time, I did not care about either of those topics. The next fad was purses. I did not own any, so I could not enter the conversation. Basically, I had nothing to talk about.

But like anything else, things changed. Eventually, my friend Valencia and I became cheerleaders at the Boys and Girls Club. Of course, I was required to have a uniform. That time, my grandmother consented to buying my uniform because she received a discount and was able to make payments. To get to practice, my friend's mother would pick me up. Other times, I had to walk over an hour to get to the Club, which was on the southside of Pomona.

Although my grandmother agreed to purchase the required cheer uniform, the same was not true for the shoes. The coach told everyone to purchase Keds. However, my grandmother took me to Payless Shoe Source to buy black tennis shoes. The difference between the two pairs of shoes is Keds have non-slip soles while the Payless shoes do not.

These Hands

As we prepared for our next competition, we looked forward to it with great anticipation because it was being televised. On the day of the event, I was having a great time, and I was doing well. That is... until I performed a high kick. With my leg in the air, my other foot slipped right from under me, and there I went... falling on my tailbone. People who watched the competition told my grandmother I did a great job despite the fall. My grandmother was happy to hear it, and she took the blame for the incident, understanding it was due to the less-expensive shoes. Nevertheless, I was so embarrassed that I ended up quitting cheer. Through it all, I enjoyed the engagement of being involved in cheer, and I obtained a couple of second-place trophies and had the opportunity to participate in a couple of city parades.

By the next year, my grandmother had loosened the reigns around me, leaving me free to roam here and there. One day, I was bike riding with a friend of mine. She wanted to go to the Boys and Girls Club to see her boyfriend. When we arrived, his brother was there as well. We all played basketball for a while. Then, we left the Club and went to the boys' home where they smoked marijuana in a pipe. They offered it to my friend and me. She accepted, but I declined the invitation. At that time, we were all in one room together, but not long after, my friend ending up leaving me and her boyfriend in his bedroom, while she and his brother went next door to his brother's bedroom.

Her boyfriend was visibly devastated by her action. He said, "Maybe she doesn't like me because my d**k is small. Do you want to see?" I told him I did not want to see. Ignoring my response, he unzipped his pants and showed me anyway. He was right; it was small. Trying to keep a straight face, I tried to encourage him by saying, "Maybe you haven't hit puberty yet." I told him I learned boys may not hit puberty until they are eighteen and that he should be patient. He said, "I hope it's sooner than that because my brother is going to be taking all my girlfriends because his is bigger than mine." Then, he said, "Let's go see what that they are doing." Next, we went into his closet because he wanted to look into his brother's room to see what they were doing. The closet was shared between the two rooms.

Looking into his brother's room from the closet, we saw the expected. My friend was in bed with his brother. Seeing that, he asked me if I wanted to have sex with him. I said, "No, I want to leave." However, that did not occur. My friend and I ended up spending the night at their home. The next morning, we left, and my friend told me to say we were at her friend Sabrina's house. Sabrina was a friend who did not exist.

When we arrived to my friend's home, she told her mother the lie, and her mother knew she was lying. When her mother drove me home, she asked me where we were. As I was unaccustomed to lying, I told the truth. It goes without saying that my friend was upset with me and did not talk to me after that even though we still saw each other at school. I asked my grandmother if I had done the right thing. She said, "Yes. Never lie for someone; you're gonna learn in life that you don't have friends anyway."

These Hands

As time progressed, not much changed in my life. I was still a loner and was still being called into the office at the middle school like I had been at the elementary school. The psychologist thought I was smoking cigarettes because my clothes constantly reeked of smoke. While I was in her office, she asked questions about my mother and father. While the questions were being fired at me, all I could hear was my grandmother's voice warning me to "not tell the white folks" our business. I did not say much, but I did tell the psychologist I was worried about my mother.

Hearing my concerns was not surprising. It was evident that something was wrong with me because my grades of A's and B's had dropped to B's and C's. My mother was still in and out of our home, and I was growing more and more embarrassed because people around town knew who she was, and she had a bad reputation of owing people money. So, I stopped telling people who my mother is.

Meanwhile, my passion for sports and physical activities continued. And, I continued to thrive in them. I continued playing basketball. I also played softball for a little while until the coach was fired for an allegation of sexual abuse involving a student. Additionally, I played soccer, which helped me gain skills for other sports, and I ran track for a spell, only participating in local track meets, never going to CIF. During summer camp at Cal Poly, I learned to swim. Overall, it was an exciting experience, but I was embarrassed when I wore my bathing suit because I was still underdeveloped. Despite my inner feelings, the coach was impressed with my swimming abilities and asked me to join the swim team. As was the standard response, my grandmother did not want to pay the fees.

In eighth grade, I wanted to continue playing basketball. Tryouts were required. I attended the first two days of tryouts; however, on the evening of the second day of tryouts, my menstrual cycle began for the very first time. I told my grandmother, and she gave me permission to stay home the next day. Missing school caused me to miss the third day of tryouts. It was required for all who wanted to make the team to be present for all three days of tryouts. When I returned the following day, the coach would not allow me to be on the team. Some of the other girls asked the coach to give me a chance. Finally, she relented and scheduled a fourth day of tryouts. I tried out and made the team.

We were having a good season when we found ourselves engaged in a close game. During that game, I had no points and had not made any shots because I was shooting with one hand, like my coach had been trying to teach me, telling me I should not shoot with two hands. With 2.3 seconds left in the game, the score was tied. Someone passed me the ball. Fully concentrating, I lifted the ball in the air with two hands. As the ball traveled from my hands to the basket, the crowd was completely silent- until the 'swoooosh' sounded, letting everyone know I had made the shot, causing us to win the game. The crowd went wild. Leaving the stadium, everyone, including the coach, the team, and fans, came to congratulate me, as our team remained undefeated.

These Hands

All that week, the volleyball coaches bowed down to me as I walked through the school. Up to that game, I was not well-known because I was a loner. But after that, everyone knew who I was. I started branching out a little more after that. For example, I began noticing and becoming interested in boys. In particular, I was interested in the star of the boys' basketball team.

As the school year was coming to a close, we closed out our basketball season with our final fundraiser- selling delicious brownies. The brownies were so good that the members of the basketball team kept buying them and eating them instead of selling them to others.

Outside of basketball, a ditch party was being planned. One of my associates convinced me to go to a ditch party, telling me the guy I liked would be there. I was excited because I knew he liked me too because we had been talking on the phone quite a bit, even falling asleep on the phone late at night, not wanting to be the first to hang up. My grandmother would get upset because I was tying up her line, so sometimes she would make me get off the phone.

When I went to the ditch party at the girl's house, the girl was in the room with a boy, and I went into another room with the boy I liked. We shared our first kiss as he lay on a bean bag and I lay on top of him. Meanwhile, some kids burst through the door, finding us fully clothed. After that, I was teased for being "weak" because I had not undressed and engaged in intercourse with him. I decided to leave and go home. On the way home, I had to duck and dodge, dipping through various yards to keep from being seen. Apparently, the principal had learned of the ditch party and was driving through the neighborhood, looking for students. The ditch party had ended, and I eventually made it home safely without being detected.

While my school life was going topsy-turvy, my home life was growing more and more concerning. One evening, a man knocked on our apartment door. When my grandmother answered, the man said, "I want to see my daughter." After he was gone, I asked, "Who was that?" My grandmother told me the man was my mother's friend, and he was asking for me. She said, "Your mother is not here, and no one needs to speak to you while she's gone." That encounter occurred more than once, and a few times, my grandmother called the police, hoping that would stop the visits.

When my mother returned home from jail, my grandmother told her about the man coming over to our home on numerous occasions. One day, my mother told me I would meet the man and that the man was indeed my father. After officially meeting my father, I began to spend time with him, my stepmother, and my siblings on weekends here and there. My father was the same man I had met some time before, when I had gone home with the two boys who had said they were my brothers.

Spending time with them was always a blast. We would roll down the streets in grocery carts, racing one another. The girls would be in one basket, and the boys would push us. Having brothers and a little sister meant a lot to me. Then, to increase our fun time in the summer, we would save up seventy-five cans each, so we could go to Ganesha Park and swim. The cans served as our entrance fee.

In the course of spending time with my father, I met his side of the family. I have six uncles and one aunt, along with a host of cousins. In the midst of meeting everyone, I met my paternal grandmother. She took a liking to me right away, even though she did not hesitate to tell me, "I don't know if you are mine or not. I'm just going by what my son told me." Hearing her words were pretty much taken as a non-factor because as long as my father had accepted me, no one else's opinion mattered. She even bought me some clothes and told my father that she wanted to take me with her to our family reunion. However, my maternal grandmother did not consent to me traveling out of state, so there went that idea and the new clothes with it.

Then, the junior prom was coming up, and the guy I liked and I had made plans to attend the dance together, but he had called a few days before and told me he had decided not to go. I took it in stride but decided to go anyway. Letting my dad know about the dance, he wanted to participate. However, my maternal grandmother did not want me to go to the prom for fear that I would end up pregnant like my older cousin. My dad convinced her to let me go, ensuring her he would have me home at a decent hour. (And, he did.) When she finally agreed, I borrowed a dress from a girl at school who lived in our complex. That same girl styled my hair in a bunch of Shirley Temple curls, and you guessed it- I looked all of ten years old. My dad picked me up and took me to his mother's house.

Before I left for the dance, he and my paternal grandmother gave me a lecture about not letting the snake crawl in the grass. Then, everyone cheered me on as my dad walked me to the car. When I arrived to the dance, I saw the guy there with an older girl. Knowing he lied to me made me feel as though I was not old enough or experienced enough for him. All the boys from school surrounded him, giving him his props for having an older girl there.

The next year, I transitioned into high school, starting ninth grade. I continued playing basketball. However, rather than playing with the other freshman and sophomores on the junior varsity team, I played with juniors and seniors on the varsity team. Many of the seniors were infuriated because they expected priority, but the coach saw fit to give priority to those who had the better skill set.

Although basketball went well for the majority of the year, by the end of the year, I was still being teased for being a virgin. I guess losing one's virginity was the thing to do. But, not for me. I was not in a hurry. I wanted to take my time and make my own decision. I was not going to be pressured by my peers.

When I was ready, I attempted to lose my virginity to a football player, but it didn't work out. He attempted, but he kept saying he couldn't because I was too small. So, he asked if I was hungry. He made us fried bologna sandwiches with Miracle Whip. So, instead of it being my first time for intercourse, it was my first time for Miracle Whip.

After it was all said and done, the boy lied and said we did actually have sex. One of my uncles heard the rumors that were being spread around, and he decided to get involved. He gave me a bit of great advice by saying, "If you are going to choose someone, choose someone who has something going for himself."

Meanwhile, I was still braiding hair, branching out a little. I was still braiding my cousin's hair, and she began to request I braid her friends' hair as well. Although I braided her hair at no charge, she required her friends to pay me, and she set the prices. Meanwhile, my grandmother was still not agreeable to paying for my basketball shoes. That time though, I was able to pay for them myself, by using the money I was making from braiding hair. Most days, I walked to school at 4am to make it to practice, which was at 6am. When my coach got wind of how far I was walking and how early, she would pick me up and take me to practice. She was happy to do it, but she reminded me of the dangers that could occur during those hours. At the end of the basketball season, our team went to CIF, but we lost.

Over the summer, I overheard a girl and boy singing in the apartment complex that was across from mine, and I asked the girl to teach me how to sing out. I already knew how to sing the falsetto. We went inside her apartment and began practicing. Then, we met back up with the boy in his apartment, and I learned he was selling drugs. I asked him how I could get in because I wanted to make more money. I was tired of going without, and I wanted to buy name brand shoes. My grandmother shopped at low-budget stores, such as Payless and

Newberry. I was becoming more accustomed to the higher end items from the kids at school, so I wanted to be able to buy them on my own. I was not making enough money from braiding to shop where I wanted to because I was only braiding at low prices, so I was searching for another option to make money, and selling drugs seemed to be a viable option.

The boy hooked me up, cutting the rocks and wrapping them for me. In that condition, I would not be required to touch them. I sold drugs for a couple of months, slanging pre-cut $20 rocks. One night while I was at the spot, the guy and girl were singing a duet, and some of the homies were freestyling. I saw a branch on the ground and picked it up from pure boredom and began swinging it around, doing old cheerleading routines, as if though the branch was a flag.

While waiting for the big homie to bring our next supply, I ended up falling asleep and spending the night there. The next day, when I awoke, after I washed my face, I saw my branch. Once again, I began doing twirls with it.

Growing bored, I walked into the living room to see if the big homie had made it over the night before. The house was very quiet, and I assumed everyone was still asleep. When I reached the living room, five police officers shouted, "Drop it!" They all had their guns aimed directly at me. I quickly dropped the branch. A female officer took me outside while asking me, "Why are you here?" Before I answered her question, I saw the homies on the floor with their hands behind their backs. I could have been shot in an instant by swinging that branch. Catching my breath, I said, "I was babysitting while they went to the store." "Where do you live?" she asked. "I live across the street," I answered.

Next, the other officers raided the apartment, finding drugs in the closet. The guys were arrested and taken to jail. Another officer questioned me. Again, I said I was just babysitting. My grandmother came over to retrieve me, and the officer told her to watch the families I babysat for. When we arrived inside our apartment, my grandmother asked if I was on drugs. I told her, "No, I was babysitting."

CHAPTER FOUR
Oh, Baby!

The summer between ninth and tenth grades was uneventful for the most part. From time to time, I hung out with a few gangbangers. But, no need for detail. Some things are best left untold.

When tenth grade began, I started off doing what I had done for a couple of years prior: attending basketball practice. While my world was essentially the same, my grandmother's world was slowly changing. Some days after practice, I would arrive home and find my grandmother passed out. She would either be lying straight back on her bed or she would be slumped over on the couch. Her skin would be sweaty and clammy. Not knowing what was wrong, I would call the paramedics, and based on my description of the situation, the operator told me to find something sweet like candy to put in her jaw and to watch her until the paramedics arrived. Once she came back to, she would react as if all was well, but I was extremely concerned. I had no idea what was causing her to pass out, and if she knew, she was not divulging any information.

Each time I would find her passed out, I would not go to school the next day because I was unsure of her condition, and I did not want anything to happen while I was away. Eventually, after my grandmother was seen by paramedics on three occasions and the paramedic told me my grandmother suffered from diabetes and that she needed to change her diet and take insulin, I stopped going to school all together. At that point, I had only completed three months of tenth grade.

Eventually, my grandmother saw her primary physician who ran a battery of tests on her. Via a phone call, my grandmother was told she was diabetic and required insulin injections. I took on the responsibility of caring for my grandmother because her insurance plan did not cover the costs of a nurse coming to the home to administer insulin every day. Furthermore, my grandmother refused to administer it herself. So, I was left with the responsibility. I administered her insulin shots daily, and I kept quiet about it because she did not want anyone to know.

As I cared for her, I was no longer participating in basketball due to my extended absence from school, and of course, my grades dropped due to absenteeism and missing work. However, I continued to braid. Girls from school would come over to have their hair braided along with my cousin and her friends. Braiding hair was and still is my stress relief. Then, to add to our household, my cousin (who had lived with us years before) brought her two children over (a girl and boy) to live with us. Somewhere along the way, she became hooked on drugs and could no longer care for her children on her own. She left them to my grandmother, but the reality was, she left them to me. My grandmother could barely take care of herself. Taking care of two young children was a bit much for her, so I shouldered the responsibility. I couldn't cook, but I kept their hair styled and helped them to get dressed.

My grandmother was adjusting to her condition and finally agreed to learn to give herself the injections. In my mind, I was free to go back to school because she had begun to control her diabetes by taking the insulin. When I attempted to return to school, I was told by school personnel I could not return because I had missed too many days. In a nutshell, I was turned away from school without any inkling of where to go and how to continue my education.

From my limited body of knowledge, I had nowhere to turn. I lacked information on alternative education formats. With no other viable options, I returned home, and there I stayed-home with my grandmother and my young cousins, braiding when I could. When I realized they were there for the long haul, I gave them my bedroom, and I took the couch. After all, there were two of them and one of me.

To help relieve my stress and to give me an outlet, my brother Jacob Jr. would call me to invite me to visit the family in Rialto. He told me how to catch the bus from Pomona to Rialto. A few weekends here and there, I would go to Rialto to visit my sister and brothers who were then living with their mother, Shonna. At that time, Shonna and our father Jacob had split up, and he was residing in Upland.

On the weekends that I visited my siblings, I had a lot of fun even though the house was overly crowded. Not only did Shonna and her five children live in the home, Shonna's brother, his girlfriend, and their children lived there as well. My brother and I smoked, drank, and had loads of fun.

Not much later, Shonna was planning to move her family to a larger house with four bedrooms, and she invited me to move with them, ensuring me she could enroll me in school once I relocated. I consented and told my grandmother I was moving out. I continued to braid to support myself.

Our house was the party house due to the size of the house and the backyard. On many occasions, we would invite family over and eat, drink, and be merry. At the house parties, I was introduced to members of Shonna's side of the family, and they were just as accepting of me as she was. They even began to get their hair braided and refer others.

On one particular occasion, I was dancing and demonstrating my flexing skills, just having a great time. Later, I went upstairs to use the restroom. The way the house was built, everyone else was downstairs on the opposite side of the house. When I came out of the bathroom, two guys, who were invited to the festivities, were along the stairwell waiting for me. One was positioned near the bedroom, at the top of the stairs. The other was standing at the bottom of the stairs, seemingly to stop me from going down.

The one near the top of the stairs grabbed my wrist as I attempted to go down the stairs. I yanked my wrist from his grip. He grabbed me again. I yanked away. That little tug of war went on for a while. Finally, I ran down the stairs and back to the party. I told Shonna what had transpired, and that night, I slept in her bed with her with the bedroom door locked. The two guys spent the night, so Shonna kept me close by for safe keeping.

Another time, one of those same two guys was at the house spending the night again. I just happened to be on my menstrual cycle, and the undergarments I was wearing became soiled. Rather than washing them, I opted to throw them away. The next morning, I went to call my siblings to come in the dining room and kitchen, so they could eat breakfast. When I walked back into the kitchen, the guy had removed the soiled undergarment from the trashcan and was holding them gingerly up to his nose. I was immediately grossed out by his behavior. Again, I reported the incident to Shonna. However, I don't know if she ever spoke to him about his actions.

My sixteenth birthday was one I will never forget. After Sunday worship service, the youth pastor drove his mother (our pastor's wife) and me to a restaurant. She and I went inside, while he pulled away, allowing us private time to celebrate our birthdays, which is on the same day, February 10. The meal was delicious, and the conversation was pleasant.

Of everything the first lady said to me, what I remember most is her discussing my daily attire. She told me unequivocally that my dress was seductive and could send the wrong message to onlookers, particularly men. She told me if I did not want to send the wrong message, I should consider wearing clothes that were less seductive and revealing. I took her words to heart, understanding that she was only speaking in my best interest. Once our meal was completed, Pastor Nathan came back to the restaurant, paid for our bill, and drove us home. I am thankful that the first lady of our church thought enough of me to impart words of wisdom into my life.

As time progressed, two things occurred. First, I began to shift my attire because I was receiving too much unwanted attention. Instead of wearing dresses, often times I opted for jeans or sweatpants. Second, we began attending church on a regular basis. Every Sunday, my siblings and I were there, and we joined the choir. At church, I met a boy named Tyler, and we began dating. Next, we moved from the four-bedroom house to a three-bedroom house in Rialto. Again, Shonna had her own room, all the boys shared a room, and my younger sister and I shared a room.

Finally, I was able to enroll in school again. My brother Jake (who was born the same year I was) and I enrolled into an alternative education school. We attended classes Monday through Thursday. Meanwhile, our older brother, Jacob Jr. was working with a guy named Isaac, with whom he carpooled. They worked the graveyard shift, so sometimes, Isaac would spend the night at our home. During that time, Isaac and I developed feelings for one another and began dating. Tyler and I had broken up, and I had moved on. Despite how I felt about Isaac, my father thought he was too old for me. He was eighteen, and I was fifteen. So, my father forced me to end the relationship. Later, I found out Tyler and Isaac not only knew each other, but they were best friends.

My relationship with Isaac turned a few people against me, such as Tyler's sister because at one time, she had dated Isaac. Also, a few other people were against me because of the relationship between Tyler and Isaac, but I had no way of knowing they knew each other. That did not seem to matter to people; they disliked the fact that I had dated both guys.

Through both the relationships, I was still attending school with the intent on catching up on my credits. One day, a very handsome young man named Logan who I never thought would say anything to me, said something slick. His words caught me off guard. Before I knew it, he was asking me for my phone number. I gave it to him. Later I found out, when he first saw me (which was some time before), he was going to ask for my number for a friend of his because he thought I was younger than I actually was. When he found out my true age, he was going to ask for himself, but I paid him no attention.

When I arrived home that afternoon and before I could clear the doorway, Shonna handed me the phone saying, "You have a phone call." From that phone call forward, we dated. In his car, he drove me everywhere- to the movies, playing pool, basketball, and all around the city. Despite all the fun we were having, dating him at times was a headache because he was very popular throughout Rialto, and all the girls wanted him. At times, the drama was too much. At the same time though, we were very compatible. I braided; he cut hair. I loved sports; and, so did he. He was the male version of me. Not only were the girls on his jock, but his mother was trying to keep him close to home. She even tried setting him up with another girl who lived closer to their home. But, my home was becoming more and more his home, as he was spending the night over there often.

Some months later, we lost the house. My younger siblings went to live with our father, and I went back to live with my maternal grandmother and my two young cousins. The relationship with Logan eventually faded out after I moved back to Pomona. Despite it all, we all continued going to church by way of the church van. One thing I learned at church was praying for others. I began to apply that concept to my life.

At church, there were guys all around. I began dating a guy named Owen, and even though I liked him as a person, I never saw us really working out because our family backgrounds were completely different. To me, it was trying to mix oil and water. He lived in a household with his two parents, who were married, along with his other siblings. I, on the other hand, came from a dysfunctional family.

During the brief dating between Owen and myself, feelings grew strong and quickly. We were not sexually active, but there was a proposal. He had made arrangements with my brother and purchased me an engagement ring. My brother rented a car and picked us up for what I thought was a date. At the end of the date, my brother drove us to the top of the hill overlooking the city. It was all beautiful. When I turned around, to my surprise, Owen was down on one knee. He proposed. I said yes, as tears streamed from my eyes.

But, just as things had happened quickly, things changed just as fast. Owen received a football scholarship to an out-of-state college. Even though he planned to leave the state, he wanted us to continue our relationship, but I did not feel confident about moving out of state. Also, there was pressure about our faithfulness in a long-distance relationship. On top of that, he was going to be around plenty of women who had similar or greater goals than his, and I hadn't even graduated high school. So, I broke things off and wished him blessings and success.

While all of my dating drama was occurring, my mother was incarcerated. Prior to going to jail, she had become pregnant. We were surprised because she had her tubes tied a few years after giving birth to me. When the time came for her to deliver, she was still incarcerated. So, she delivered her baby in jail on May 31, 1997. My grandmother was called to retrieve the child, which was a baby girl. If she failed to do so, the baby would have gone into the foster care system. Of course, my grandmother did not desire foster care for any of her grandchildren, so she immediately went to the jail in Riverside to pick up her newest grandchild.

Meanwhile, I continued to visit Logan off and on even though I had moved on emotionally due to all the drama with him and other girls. It was really just a physical attraction that kept me coming around. Finally, I made up my mind to discontinue our encounters. One night in November 1997, I went to his sister's home to visit him, knowing it would be my last time seeing him because I was ready for a change.

We hung out and ate nachos at a nearby Mexican food joint. Later, we engaged in intercourse. Afterwards, he hopped up and went to the restroom. He came back and said he had bad news. I asked what it was, and he said the condom had broken. I was shocked. He was the one who had provided the condom, so I asked him if it was an old one because I found it unusual for them to break. I asked to see it, but he said he had flushed it. I did not believe him. Later, we showered and went to sleep.

In the middle of the night, as he was still sleeping, I left and went back to my grandmother's house. A few hours later, I had a strange feeling, so I went to the bathroom. Upon wiping myself, on the tissue lay the tip of the condom. At that point, I knew he had not been lying. I finishing cleaning and left it at that.

Late January of the new year, I had decided to move to my aunt-in-law's house in Lancaster, so I could go back to school. While I was with my aunt, she noticed my everyday behaviors were slightly altered. Specifically, she said I was sleeping more than normal. She asked if I was pregnant. I told her I was not. She wanted proof positive, so she took me to a doctor for a pregnancy test. The test came back positive. I was eleven weeks along.

The test results halted my plan of going back to school. Furthermore, school would have been difficult to achieve despite the pregnancy because I was helping my grandmother take care of my little sister. Back to my grandmother's house I went, to my grandmother, my little sister, and my two little cousins. It was a bit crowded, but we made the best of it.

Social services paid us a visit regarding my baby sister. They wanted to put her in the system, basically saying my grandmother was too old to care for an infant and I was not eighteen yet. And being pregnant did not make it any better. It became imperative to find someone who could care for my little sister on a full-time basis. Otherwise, she would be required to go into the foster care system. First, we checked with my paternal grandmother. She was willing to assist. One of her requirements though was for my maternal grandmother to release the check she was receiving on my sister's behalf to my paternal grandmother. My grandmother refused. She had agreed to purchase everything the baby needed, but she would not surrender the entire check.

Next, we inquired with my aunt-in-law. She agreed to care for my sister until I turned eighteen. That sounded like a good plan, so we gave it a go. Later, to prevent my sister from going into the foster care system, my aunt adopted her and raised her until she was eighteen. That took away my option of raising my sister once I turned eighteen, and there was nothing I could do about it.

Eventually, everyone in the family learned of my pregnancy. I moved from my maternal grandmother's house to live

These Hands

with my paternal grandmother and an aunt, who had taken it upon herself to teach me how to prepare for and raise the baby. I learned about government assistance and signed up for the program, so I could have money and food for my baby. Once I began to receive the money, I paid rent to my grandmother for the room I shared with my uncle and covered the phone bill.

Life moved on, and my belly became enlarged. Although I was no longer dating the father of my baby at that time, my mother had insisted I call him to inform him of my pregnancy. I did not want to, for I had broken contact with him, and I anticipated his response. At first, I did not understand her reasoning or her insistence. She explained, "You need to tell him about the baby. I did not tell you about your father. Don't do that to your baby." Taking her advice, I told Logan about the pregnancy. Just as I had anticipated, he stated, "It ain't mine." I replied, "Well, I know it's mine!" I did not wait for any further replies. I disconnected the call. He was at my grandmother's door the next day to be accepting of our baby.

Months before it was time to give birth, I had thought with everything going on in my life that school was no longer an option for me. I was wrong. I did re-enroll in school, attending an alternative school. However, my school exploits would be short lived.

On August 24, 1998, I received a call from the hospital, explaining my due date had passed on the 19th. However, I had not begun having contractions. During the phone call, I was asked if I would like to be induced that evening. I agreed. I asked my older brother to take a walk with me. He agreed, and for a walk we went. He had no idea I was walking to the hospital to be induced. I wanted to be alone and not tell anyone, but my brother said he had to tell my grandmother because he would have no explanation of where I went. Upon our arrival, he stayed for a while; then, he left.

Nine hours after being induced, I delivered a beautiful healthy baby girl on August 25th. Her dad, his mother, father and sister were all there. My grandmother and aunt were there as well. I felt as though they just wanted to see if my baby looked like her father at all, given the situation.

After the delivery, I was starving. My grandmother had brought me a complete meal of fried catfish, greens, and hot water cornbread. I loved her hot water cornbread. The next day, Logan came to drive me and our daughter home.

As my baby grew, days turned into weeks, and weeks into months. Her father would come the house to visit her, but he would end up in the backyard with my family members, drinking and smoking. During his visits, we would sometimes spend private time together. We had a rendezvous that led to another pregnancy when our daughter was three months. I elected not to continue the pregnancy.

As life progressed, I developed my craft along with my clientele. My aunt who was living with us was also a braider. I would braid in my bedroom, and she would braid in hers. On one occasion, one of my aunt's clients saw a style I was braiding and decided she was going to call me the next time to braid her hair, so she could have that particular style. When my aunt found out about it, she told my grandmother. From that point forward, my grandmother required I pay her $10 for every person's hair I braided.

The incidents between my aunt and me did not stop with the braiding incident. When my daughter was five months old, my aunt's daughter, who was five years old, wanted to give my daughter a bath. I told her I would help her bathe my daughter. My little cousin began to cry because she wanted to give the bath on her own. With my daughter being an infant and my cousin only being five, I could not allow it. My aunt grew upset and told my grandmother about the incident. Their voices were elevated as they discussed me. My grandmother said, "Maybe, she is jealous. Maybe, she thinks her baby is special." I interrupted by asking, "Jealous about what?" Needless to say, no one responded to my question.

The only thing that made sense to me regarding my aunt's negative attitude towards me was a request she had made to my brother. She had asked him to buy her son a jacket. In response, he stated, "No, your son has a father. I'm shopping for my niece." He was referring to my daughter. It caused a scene, but I was no longer a confrontational person. So, I let it go.

After the continued incidents, I thought it best to move. I was moving on with life, and I was trying to be a better me for me and my daughter. And, I had noticed a change within myself. After my daughter's birth, I had become more compassionate toward others. Basically, she had made me soft.

CHAPTER 5

From Sin Town to Sin City

When I decided to move from my paternal grandmother's house, I moved to Pomona to once again live with my maternal grandmother and my two young cousins who continued to reside there. That time, my stay would be for approximately one month. At that time, my mother was still in and out of jail and was not financially independent.

One day, a taxi pulled up to the house, and my mother stepped out. Quickly, she ran into the house, trying to avoid paying the taxi driver. The taxi driver, however, did not drive away and take his loss in stride. Instead, he came to the front door and demanded his money. As I frequently did, I covered my mother's expenses, using money I had made from braiding. When my grandmother saw what had transpired, she began to go off on my mother telling her, "You can't keep doing this to her. She has a new baby to take care of."

In her defense, my mother said, "I was just trying to get home. It was too cold to walk." For me, the situation was nothing. I had grown accustomed to helping my mother out in her times of need. However, I wasn't sure if I was doing the right thing or not by always coming to her rescue. I decided to talk to my older brother about it. I know the Bible says to honor our mother and father, but I didn't know if giving her money was honoring her or not. My brother's advice to me was to go to church on a regular basis to get a better understanding of God's Word.

Approximately one week later, I took my daughter Princess to see her father and her grandparents. While I was there, my grandmother called me and told me my mom had just returned home... from the hospital. We had no idea she had been in the hospital. We only knew she hadn't been at home. But, that was normal. She ended up in the hospital because she had been beaten badly to the point where her eyes would not open and fluid was leaking from her ear, which was supposedly fluid from the brain. When I asked her what happened, she said a group of Mexicans jumped her. That was all the information she would divulge. For the next few weeks, I had to take her back-and-forth to the doctor's office to make sure she was healing properly.

After getting my mother back on the road to recovery, I thought about what my brother said about going to church. Not having a car of my own, I was required to ride the church van as a means of getting there. So, one of the deacons would come over and pick me up and also pick up my brother Jacob Jr. from his house, so we could attend services.

On one Saturday, there was an event at church, and the deacon picked us up to take us to the event. Because church was the next day, it was suggested that we spend the night at the deacon's house with his wife and family and then go to church the next morning, so he wouldn't have to drop us off in the evening and pick us back up in the morning. My brother and I decided that would be a good idea, so he, my baby daughter, and I spent the night in one of their son's bedroom, who just so happened to be my ex-boyfriend Owen. Owen was not home, so his room was vacant because he had run away with the girl he was dating after our breakup. He had been gone for nearly two weeks. Owen was one of the guys I had briefly dated when I attended the church before.

In the room was a king-size bed, so my brother, my daughter, and I slept on the bed together. In the middle of the night, I was awakened to my panties having already been slid over, feeling slight penetration. I was quickly feeling confused because the last thing I knew there was only my brother, me, and my daughter in the room. When I became focused and realized what was going on and who it was, I felt a second penetration, then wetness. While I was lifting myself up to push him back, I asked, "What are you doing?" Then, I pushed him again. His reply was, "I still love you. I'm sorry."

At that moment, we heard movement and a door opening down the hallway. He said, "Lay down. That's my mom." I did what he suggested even though I knew how it would look to anyone who walked in. He quickly moved to the other side of the bed where my brother was lying down. We both pretended to be asleep. His mother came into the room and placed oil on our foreheads, as part of her morning prayer ritual. When she saw her son in the room with us, she grunted when she saw her son in room. When the coast was clear, I got up and went downstairs and showered. I remained downstairs on the couch to keep away from my ex.

Not too much longer after that incident, I moved from Pomona to San Bernardino to live with Jacob Jr. and Shonna. The arrangement was for me to pay half the rent and one of the bills, and Shonna would take care of the other half of the rent and the other bills. Shonna worked in L.A. at a bakery, and every weekend, she rode the Metrolink home, bringing our younger siblings, who resided with our dad, with her. So basically, the apartment would be Jacob and mine alone during the week. When she came home, she brought cakes, cupcakes, cheesecakes, and all sorts of goodies from the bakery. They were always delicious- until I got sick. I thought I had consumed too much sugar or something.

A couple of months later, I learned I was pregnant as a result of the events that occurred at the deacon's house. I was twelve weeks along. At first, I didn't tell anyone about my pregnancy. But, on one Sunday at church, one of the youths came up to me and asked me if I was pregnant. I told her I was, and I asked her how she knew. She said Owen had told one person he thought he had gotten me pregnant, and that person told another, and the second person told another, and so on, and so on.

Eventually, the words got back to the adults. Owen's father, the deacon who drives the bus, came up to me and asked me if I was pregnant. Because he was an adult, I admitted that I was. After that, it seemed as though everyone in Owen's family, except for those around my age, stopped talking to me.

To me, everyone was waiting to see what was going to happen, if the baby I would give birth to was truly their family member or not. What was most hurtful to me was hearing words about how I got pregnant on purpose as if I wanted something from their family. Eventually, I stopped going to church.

Meanwhile, my ex-boyfriend Isaac had come back to California from Vegas. He had moved to Vegas a couple of years before, and I had not seen him since we dated when I was fifteen years old. He saw everything I was going through, and he felt really bad about how I was being treated. He told me, "If you were pregnant by me, I wouldn't treat you the way you're being treated." I was in a really vulnerable state, and the attention he was giving me made me feel special, loved, and wanted. When I was around him, I did not feel like an outcast. After some time went by, Isaac had visited me so many times at my home that he ended up living with us. Sometime later, we ended up losing the apartment because the owners wanted to sell the building. So, Isaac, Jacob Jr., Princess, and I ended up moving with my father in Upland with all of my other siblings.

When I was five months pregnant, my daughter was turning a year old. I had a birthday party for her at a park, and Logan came. It was on that day that he learned that I was pregnant by someone else and about me dating Isaac. It was then that he began to be less present in our daughter's life. Thankfully, his mother remained active. She did not miss a beat. She was also accepting of Isaac. She said she did not have a problem with him helping to raise her granddaughter.

Living with my father and siblings, had its ups and downs. My oldest brother and my father ended up having a disagreement leading to Jacob Jr. moving out. Then, my sister was exhibiting strange behavior. For example, when Isaac would be in the bathroom showering, she would go in to use the bathroom. I would question her about it, and she would just say, "Well, I need to use the bathroom," as if it was no big deal for a fifteen-year-old girl to go into the bathroom while a naked man was in there.

Then, to put more of a strain on life itself, Isaac was tired of having on and off again jobs with the temp agency. He wanted more stability. So, he asked me to move to Vegas with him. There were other factors that led him to wanting to leave California, specifically my dad's house.

For one, we couldn't save money because in addition to giving my dad money for the rent and food, we also were assisting with buying my younger brothers and sister backpacks, clothing, and other things they needed.

Secondly, on one particular day, I drove Isaac to work, so I could use the car to pick up my dad from his job at the fair. On the way back from the fair, a police officer pulled us over, and the car ended up being towed for lack of registration or something of that sort. Without having a car, Isaac was unable to get to work at UPS, so he ended up losing his job.

The situation at home became more tense. On one occasion, my dad needed extra money once again. That time it was for the electricity bill, for which we had already given him money, but apparently, he spent it and was asking for it again with the threat that the lights were going to be shut off. Isaac told my father that it was not our responsibility to keep giving him money. There was no way we could save while giving him the majority of our money. They went back-and-forth over and over again until the argument turned into a physical altercation. My father told Isaac he needed to leave. Then, he looked at me and said I could stay, but if I stayed, the bill needed to be paid.

After that, Isaac moved to Vegas, to go find work, which he quickly did. I moved back to Pomona once again with my maternal grandmother. I was thankful that regardless of whatever I was going through, I could always go back home. While Isaac was in Vegas working, I was under the impression we would be moving in with his mother when he was able to send for me. Thankfully, it only took a couple of months for him to have a date for us to join him in Vegas. While I waited, I braided everyone's hair I could before the move.

The night before we were going to leave, Princess's dad came to visit her. We talked, and he expressed his concerns and frustrations, but we were still leaving. Isaac's sister drove to California from Vegas to pick up my daughter and me to join Isaac in Vegas. We were packed and ready to go. The day I moved to Vegas was my first time ever going there.

Upon our arrival, we pulled into an apartment complex. I thought it was his sister's residence, but it was a surprise. It was actually our own apartment. There was a grocery store, a mall, and a beauty supply within walking distance. They also had a job for me, so I could have income until I built up clientele. My job was to babysit Isaac's two nieces while his sister worked. That was in November 1999.

One month later, my daughter and I were home alone, and Isaac was at work. Throughout the day, I drank tea and allowed my body to relax. Early the next morning, I woke up with the urge to go to the bathroom. After I walked out of the bathroom, I walked over to where Isaac was sleeping, and all of a sudden, I felt a gush release from my body. I woke Isaac up and told him my water had broken. He first thought was to tell me, "Okay, get off the carpet." I laughed it off and went into the bathroom to take a bath.

After bathing, I got dressed, while Isaac got Princess dressed. Once he had her ready, he opened the front door and they walked out to the car, leaving me behind. Due to the excitement and adrenaline, he had forgotten all about me. I tried to catch up to them, but I had to move slowly. Eventually, he must have remembered the reason why we were going to the hospital and noticed I wasn't there. So, he came back upstairs and helped me down. Away to the hospital, we went.

Six hours later, I gave birth to a beautiful baby boy. I had not planned what his name would be, so as he lay on the table, I kept looking at him saying, "There he is." I said those three words over and over until they turned into 'Gregory.' At that point, I decided that would be his name. Then, I gave him Isaac's middle name because he had been there for him and me throughout the entire pregnancy. Then, I finalized my son's name with my last name.

The family of support that I needed was there at the hospital. That support system consisted of Isaac's family, his mother and his sisters. Upon leaving the hospital, I did not go back to our apartment. Instead, I went to Isaac's mother's house. I stayed there for a week, and she waited on me hand and foot. That is exactly what I needed at that time. Otherwise, I would have been home alone with a one-year-old little girl and a newborn, while Isaac was at work.

A few days later, Owen and his family along with my brother Jacob Jr. came to Vegas to see Gregory. As he lay on the bed, they all peered at him and said, "Yep, that's Owen's baby," noticing similar facial features between Owen and Gregory.

While Owen and his family were in Vegas, one of his aunts called us over to the Golden Nugget to have dinner with them. We went, and we all ate together. Also, during that night, the aunt told me she would send her son's old clothes to me for my baby. She did exactly what she said. She sent two large boxes of clothes to me from Atlanta, and my son did not need any clothes until he was a year and a half.

Once my son's father and his family left Vegas, I did not hear from any of them after that for a long while; however, from time to time one of my son's uncles would ask my brother about how we were doing.

After living in the apartment for a while, we eventually moved to a better neighborhood, still in Vegas. And even though things are going well, I would find myself getting homesick quite often. Therefore, I and my two children would drive to California on some weekends to visit family. Other times, Isaac, I, and the children will take the drive to California. On one particular trip, some family issues arose regarding money between two of my brothers, Jacob Jr and Jake.

Jake was so upset that he decided he could no longer live in California. So, he packed his bags and returned to Vegas with us. Upon our return, he lived with us for about a month. Then, that situation turn bad. While out at the pool one day, my brother offered a group of minors some beer. One of the children's father came to our door and told us about the incident. At that point, we had to ask Jake to leave our home. Because he had already found a job as a cook, he was able to move out with his girlfriend and get his own place. But, we didn't see much of him. One day, we ran into his girlfriend and asked her where he was. She told us they had lost their apartment, and she had not seen him since then. From there, we lost contact with him.

Around that same timeframe, Isaac found a program that pays the required fee for people to take the GED test. I was very excited because I had tried to return to school on several occasions, and nothing had worked out for me. With that opportunity, I was determined to pass. So, to prepare for the test, I used the study guide *Math for Dummies* to refresh my memory for the math portion. Then, I decided to take a practice test, to ensure I was actually ready. I passed. In March of 2000, I took the actual test. It was eight hours long and included an essay question asking, "Who would you change and why?" Answering the question, I wrote about my mother. When the results came, I received the news that I had passed the test! I was excited to have that educational part of my life behind me.

When my son became a little older, I got a job at a telephone company in the customer service department. I worked during the day while Isaac worked at night. I would have two days off during the week, and he would have weekends off. So, as you can see, our schedules didn't match up. Nevertheless, we made it work. And with the two jobs, we were able to buy a car. I was still trying to go to California as often as I could because I was growing more and more homesick by the day.

One day, while I was at work, a customer called in regarding his bill. As the customer spoke, I recognized his voice. I said, "Dad?" And he responded, "Phoebe?" We laughed. After having reconnected by an unexpected phone call at my job, we kept in touch often. But it didn't take too long for things to turn back to their old ways. He began to call me at work and tell me he didn't have money for the bill, so I found myself sending him money. Unfortunately, me sending money to California caused problems at home with Isaac. He said I was taking money out of our home to help my family, which was true.

Eventually, my homesickness won me over, and we moved back to California to the city of Rancho Cucamonga to live with one of my cousins. That cousin is the same one whose hair I used to braid when we lived in the same apartment complex when we were younger. Back in 1998, I had put in an application at that apartment complex when my daughter was just a baby. But, I never heard back. My cousin suggested I go to the office and ask the manager the status of my account. I did that, and the manager said my name was coming up soon on the list. When I had first applied, I did not know there was a three to five year waiting list. It was then 2000. While we waited for my name to come up for the apartment, we received homeless assistance, which provided us a hotel voucher for a week or two, as we looked for another place to live. Once we found a place, the homeless assistance would pay the deposit for an apartment, within a certain range. Eventually, we found a one-bedroom/one-bathroom apartment down the street from where we had lived before in San Bernardino.

Being back in California allowed me to begin braiding again. And, business picked up quickly. It was enough to support our family, as Isaac wasn't working at that time and the kids were still young.

CHAPTER 6
'Til Death Do Us Part

2000 was a good year, with the birth of my son and all that life had to bring. But, 2001 brought so many unexpected and life-altering changes that my entire world was shaken.

At that time, Shonna was living in a women's home in the city of Fontana, and she was pregnant with her sixth child. Neither of us had a car of our own, so I would borrow my cousin's car to take Shonna to her prenatal appointments. At the beginning of her pregnancy, her doctor had suggested she lose 150 pounds; otherwise, her weight could cause her to have a heart attack or a stroke. She asked her doctor how she was supposed to lose weight while she was pregnant. It was recommended that in order for her to lose weight and not allow the weight to lead to any health problems, she should terminate the pregnancy. For Shonna, that was not a viable option. She told her doctor, "No, I will not end the pregnancy. I have faith that God will see me through this pregnancy safely."

In February, Shonna was scheduled to see her obstetrician again. She called me to see if I could provide a ride for her to the doctor's office. On that particular day, my cousin was in Las Vegas, so I could not borrow her car. So, Shonna decided to ride the city bus to the doctor's office. She called me when she was getting on the bus, and she was supposed to call me when she returned back home. However, I did not hear from her.

The next night, Jacob Jr. called me and told me when Shonna had gone to see her obstetrician, her blood pressure was high. Her doctor sent her to the hospital to go directly to the emergency room. From there, she was admitted to the hospital. All of that led to an emergency C-section being performed to deliver her baby, on February 19, 2001. After her baby was delivered, Shonna was taken from the delivery room to a regular patient room where she could rest comfortably. All of that transpired without her being able to see her newborn baby boy because there were some difficulties during the birth, leading to him ingesting stool. As a result, he was sent to the neonatal intensive care unit (NICU) to have his system cleared out.

Then, sometime during the night, when a housekeeper was making her rounds, she found Shonna unresponsive. The housekeeper hit the 'cold blue' button, causing nurses and doctors to immediately arrive on the scene. They were able to resuscitate Shonna, causing her heart to once again begin pumping blood throughout the body. However, no one knew how long she had gone without oxygen. Although her heart was back functional, she was said to have minimal brain activity. At that point, she was placed on life-support.

More Than Just a Braider

The next morning, I met Jacob Jr. at the hospital. All the night before and as I drove to the hospital that morning, I couldn't help but wonder if things would have turned out differently if I had been able to take her to the hospital. For one, she would not have been alone and endured everything that had transpired. Going through that experience caused me to do all I can to be there for people in their time of need. Granted, I could not have changed the situation about not having a car, but now, I try to go the extra mile for those in need to prevent an unfortunate situation.

After I arrived to the hospital, Jacob Jr., Shonna's mother, her sisters, and I assembled in a waiting room, waiting to meet a doctor to learn what had occurred. When the doctor arrived, he told us it was a freak accident. According to him, Shonna had consumed some food, and it had become lodged in her esophagus, causing her to choke. I spoke up and told the doctor that what he was saying did not make any sense because Shonna would have been on a liquid diet, unable to consume solid foods. So, if that were the case, how could she have choked on something solid? The doctor said maybe someone sneaked some food in to her. But, no one had known she was in the hospital. Immediately, I'll began to think that something didn't sound right. Something was amiss. The doctor was already placing blame elsewhere, in an attempt for the hospital to not be liable for Shonna's condition.

The doctor's last words were for us to hope that more brain activity would develop in order for her to come off life support. Everyone who is in the room was listening to the doctor and crying heartfelt tears of sadness. Jacob Jr. immediately began praying for a good outcome, confessing what he wanted to happen with his mother, my stepmother. All of us bowed our heads in the spirit of agreement as he prayed. At the end, we all whispered, "Amen."

The next day, I went back to the hospital with my notebook in hand, so I could document everything that was said. I began to ask questions, such as what time Shonna left the delivery room to be taken to the patient room and how often her vitals were checked. I asked for the times, the dates, and the names of the people who were responsible for her care. As the days went on, Shonna's body began to swell little by little, day after day. I tried to encourage all of my brothers and my sister throughout that process. Meanwhile, I would go into Shonna's room to talk and pray with her, hoping for a response as I held her hand, hoping she would squeeze my hand in return. The only response we saw was Shonna's eyes fluttering. The doctor said the fluttering of the eyes meant nothing. It was just a bodily response that was not initiated by the words we said to her.

Throughout everything, her baby boy Dexter was still in the NICU. We were instructed to take CPR training classes in order to be able to care for him properly. We did that and received our certifications. Finally, when it was time for Dexter to be released from the hospital, he had to be released to the next of kin, which turned out to be Jacob Jr, as his father was absent from the picture. At that time, Jacob Jr. was living from place to place, so he used my address to be able to have Dexter released to him from the hospital. From there, both Jacob Jr. and Dexter came to my home to live. At that time, we were still living in my apartment in San Bernardino.

A few days after the incident, the family was called to the hospital for a meeting. The doctor was suggesting to remove Shonna from life support because her condition had not improved and her body had begun to deteriorate. Jacob Jr. was not ready to disconnect his mother from the system that was allowing her to stay alive. He requested another four days. However, Medi-Cal would only pay for the three days she had already been on. The doctor stated there was no brain activity although the heart was pumping. Eventually, Jacob Jr. came around and decided it was time to remove Shonna from life support.

During the process of disconnecting her from life support, Jacob Jr. and I stayed in the room and held her hands. After she was disconnected, the doctors suggested we leave due to the responses the body would give afterwards. They told us it was not something we wanted to witness.

As we walked from the room, I did my best to console Jacob Jr. by rubbing his back. From there, all of our discussions were about the funeral services for Shonna. We wanted to put her away peacefully. After that, our assignment would be to raise our little brother. So, to prepare for the funeral services, we began making calls to borrow money and to get donations. Thankfully, we were given a plot for Shonna to be buried in. Once all of the arrangements had been made, we had the service to say our final goodbye.

Shortly afterward, my family and I moved from San Bernardino to Alta Loma in March when my name reached the top of the list. Not long before that, my dad had moved from Upland to Fontana. When I moved to Alta Loma, Jacob Jr. and Dexter moved to Fontana with our dad and our other siblings.

Living in the new apartment was great because my cousin was there, and my children would go over there from time to time. Having family close by was wonderful. Also, my braiding business was picking up greatly. I was braiding 16 to 20 hours a day, like I had been in San Bernardino. Also, being not too far from my dad and my siblings, I could visit them on a regular basis. During that time, I was also going to church more often. I had even begun to participate in outreach on Saturdays, passing out tracks for the church, to save more souls.

Isaac and I were still getting along well as we raised my two children. To keep my child count to two, I had begun to take the Depo-Provera shot. Prior to getting the first shot, the doctor was required to administer a pregnancy test and gain a negative result. Everything went smoothly, and I was given the shot. Every three months when the shot was re-administered, a pregnancy test was given again. After having taken the shot a couple of times, I went back for my next shot and to have the anticipated pregnancy test. I was informed that I could not be given the next shot because my test had come back positive. Both my doctor and I were surprised. The doctor's advice was for me to terminate the pregnancy due to the baby having the medication in his/her system, which could lead to birth defects.

I spoke to Isaac about it extensively, and we decided to keep the baby and trust God that all would be well. I remembered Shonna having faith when the doctor had given her the advice about weight loss and her baby, so I decided to exercise my faith as well. Plus, the baby would be Isaac's first biological child, and he was very excited.

When my father learned of my pregnancy, he asked me if he could name the baby. I told him yes -as long as the baby was not named Jacob. You see, my father's name is Jacob, and my older brother, being his junior, is also named Jacob. I told him there were enough Jacob's around. He agreed to name the baby something else.

In June of that same year, Isaac and I were at home one morning, when someone came walking up to the front door. Isaac looked out and saw that it was our youth pastor, Nathan Smith. Isaac said, "Nathan is here." When Pastor Nathan entered our home, he asked us to have a seat because he needed to tell us something. At that moment, I heard, for the second time that year, the most unexpected news. Pastor Nathan began to tell us that my father had been involved in a car accident that was the catalyst of a tire blowing out. When the tire blew out, my dad lost control of the car because the steering column became disengaged, causing the car to spin out and land in a ditch.

In the vehicle were four people. My dad was driving, and in the passenger seat was his female roommate, and in the back seat directly behind my father was my father's girlfriend's daughter and in the seat behind the roommate was my father's girlfriend's son. During the spin out, my father and the thirteen-year-old girl were both ejected from the car, causing their immediate deaths. After hearing the news, my immediate response was, "Where are Perris, Jayden, and Ashton?" I needed to know where my younger siblings were and how they were doing because in the span of four months, they had lost both of their parents.

Prior to my dad's passing, he had had hip surgery at Park West Hospital. After the surgery, he noticed that his leg had been mis-measured, and one leg was then shorter than the other. As a result, he had filed suit against the hospital and had won a settlement. He was scheduled to have a second surgery, but he was fearful of doing so, not knowing what the outcome would be. He instructed Jacob Jr. that if anything should happen to him, to take the money from the settlement and to pay all of Shonna's final expenses, meaning Jacob Jr. was to use the settlement to pay back all the money that had been borrowed to ensure her a proper burial. The anticipated settlement check came after my father passed, so Jacob Jr. used the money to cover both parents' funeral expenses.

A few months later, Pastor Nathan took the youth to a gospel concert at Magic Mountain. On the way home, I began to share something that had been heavy on all my heart for quite some time. I asked Pastor Nathan, "How do you know when you have honored your parents?" He told me honoring your parents means being there for them and respecting them at all times. I began to explain to him that I was there for my parents and that I respected them. Also, I tried to take care of their needs by giving them money, but they did not always do the right thing with it. Pastor Nathan ensured me that I had done the right thing, and that it was not for me to worry about what they did with the money once they got it. Having that conversation with him gave me such peace of mind.

Through a braiding client, who is also a friend of the family, I was able to receive some much-needed information. One day, she was teaching me a new method of braiding called 'tree braiding,' and as we were going through the training session, I began to share with her that something was not right with the way Shonna had died. She suggested I contact a lawyer in Rancho Cucamonga. I did that immediately, and the lawyer started the process of investigation once I provided to her all the information I had surrounding the event.

In October, my paternal grandmother was celebrating a birthday, and Isaac, Jacob Jr., and I attended the celebration. My younger sister Perris babysat the children while we were at the party. We were having a lot of fun, but later on into the night, Isaac wanted to go home. So, we got in the car, and I drove him home. Then, I returned to the party. By the time I returned back home, it was three or four in the morning. When

Perris answered the door, she was looking frantic. When she saw us, she said she was ready to go home. I asked her what was wrong, and when Jacob Jr. saw the look on her face, he asked her the same question. She didn't answer us. Perris and Jacob Jr. left, and I went to bed.

The next day, we drove to church in the car my uncle had given to me. After church, we went to Jacob Jr.'s house to eat and fellowship. Perris came over to me and told me she had something to tell me. I said to her, "Okay, what is it?" She told me Isaac had been molesting her for some time by touching her breasts. I immediately asked her if she was okay, and she said yes she was until the night before when he pulled out his private part and placed it near her face asking her, "Are you ready?" She told him no and to get out of the room. I asked her what happened next, and she said he left and went back into our bedroom.

I immediately telephoned the police. The police officer said many claims are made when people are upset at their boyfriends, so they needed to hear the accusation directly from her. I handed her the phone, but she hung the telephone up. She said, "I just wish Daddy was here to do something to him." I asked her, "If this has been going on for a while, why didn't you tell Daddy when he was still alive? And why wait to tell me when I'm almost due? If he hurt you or made you feel uncomfortable, he needs to be in jail." She responded, "It's okay. I don't want to mess up y'all lil' happy family."

Then, I marched over to where Isaac was and asked him about what Perris had said. He said, "What? She's lying..."

Shortly after that, we left and went home. We talked about the situation again, and eventually, Isaac told me that the interaction that had occurred between them was consensual. Supposedly, Perris had begun the conversation telling him she had lost her virginity and to whom and that she felt she was ready to go further with him after all the previous moments they had of touching.

After hearing what both of them had to say, I truly did not know what to do. I was going to be raising three children, as my baby was due to be born within the next month. Isaac and I had been together for a long time, and that compounded the situation as well.

Not knowing which direction to take, I decided to speak to a few people at church. To my surprise, everyone already knew about the situation between my sister and my boyfriend. Well, at least they knew about the accusations she had made towards him. Some said the accusation came out as jealousy towards me. Also, my sister had gained a reputation for being flirtatious, so it was difficult for anyone to take her seriously. Some even claimed she had made false accusations before. In the end, I was told to not let that situation get in the way of my family. It was also advised that I stop shacking up and take my personal life more seriously, as I had younger girls of the church looking up to me.

Taking into consideration all that was said, there was one thing that greatly concerned me: I was raising a daughter in the household that was not Isaac's. If he was prone to behavior of sexual improprieties, I did not want my daughter to be exposed to that. After all was said and done, I decided to continue my relationship and remain in the home with Isaac.

The next month, on November 2, 2001, I went to Park West Hospital, while my cousin babysat Princess and Gregory. While having contractions, I walked around to help move the labor process forward. After four hours of extreme exhaustion, our son was born free of any birth defects. Before his name was decided upon, I reflected upon the conversation I had had with my father. Isaac and I discussed it, and he did not desire to have a junior, so we named our son in honor of my father and chose his middle name to honor my cousin who had lost a son when he was just an infant. That is how the name Jacob came to be.

One month later, at the end of a Sunday worship service, Isaac and I had a simple wedding, giving our vows as husband and wife. We vowed to be a family: he, I, and our three children. My brother walked me down the aisle in my father's absence. While walking, I reminisced about my dad walking me down the yard to the car when I went to the junior prom. The ceremony did not take too long and only a few were in attendance, including my son Gregory's grandmother.

Afterward, those who were there gave us hugs. My son's grandmother hugged me and whispered in my ear, "You will always be my daughter-in-law." Once all the hugs were given, Isaac and I went to eat at Red Lobster. Afterward, we went home. I did not know how to feel at that moment. I was just glad it was all over with.

CHAPTER 7
What in the Law?

When 2002 rolled in, the lawyer I had contacted was still working our case. For her to move forward and make any real progress, Jacob Jr. was required to obtain Shonna's medical records and death certificate. In the process of the investigation, we learned Shonna had suffered a massive heart attack and that she had not choked on food or anything else. The investigator was also attempting to learn why Shonna had not been placed on a heart monitor when the hospital knew she had heart problems and why a nurse wasn't checking on her more frequently.

As the investigation moved forward, life continued as normal. As I had tried before to keep my child count to a minimum, after I gave birth to my son Jacob, I decided to take a different form of birth control. That time, I tried the pill, as it had been successful for me when I was a bit younger. Nevertheless, I still became pregnant.

I was quite certain that I did not want any more children. I told my obstetrician, the same one that I had been going to for my other pregnancies, that I do not want any more kids. My body was tired, and I didn't believe it could handle another pregnancy. So, I scheduled an appointment at the abortion clinic, and both Isaac and I went.

Upon our arrival there, we were met by protesters standing outside the clinic telling us abortion was wrong. Despite their efforts, we went inside for our scheduled appointment. Before an abortion can be a performed, an ultrasound is usually done to see the stage of the fetus. I lay on the table and had the ultrasound. Then, the ultrasound technician left the room, but she left the monitor in my view. When I saw the baby moving around with legs and arms, I looked at my husband and told him I could not have the abortion.

As we left the clinic, again we had to move through the people who were outside protesting. One man looked at me and said, "Think about the babies." I responded, "I am. I'm not going to do it," referring to the abortion. The man smiled as we walked away.

I moved on from there with the full intent of continuing my pregnancy. Meanwhile, I was still braiding and attending church. Although life was pretty much the same, I had begun to keep my distance from my sister after the incident with her and Isaac. Although I didn't want to hold it against her, it was hard to erase it from my mind.

May 31, 2002 started it off like any normal day for me as a wife and mother of three young children, who was three to four months pregnant with her next child. That day, I decided to take my children to the park, so the oldest two could run around and use up their excessive energy, while I played with Jacob, who was about five months. Before going to the park, I recalled one of my clients telling me about a school that was not too far from my home. I wanted to stop by there to pick up an information brochure to learn more about what type of classes were offered.

Located next to the school building was a café. I decided to park directly in front of the café and run over to the school building to get the brochure. When I got out of my car, a woman exited the café and told me I could not park there. I look down at the parking spot to see if it was marked in any special way, only to find it was not. Looking back at the lady, I said, "Why not? It's not marked." She said, "I'm tired of people parking here. It stops my customers from coming in."

For the next few minutes, we went back and forth about whether or not I was legally able to park in that particular parking spot. I was trying to explain to the woman that I just needed a brochure from the school next door and that I could've actually gone to get it and been back and out of the parking spot all the time I had been standing there arguing with her about it. Finally, I just walked away and went to the school, leaving Princess, Gregory, and Jacob in the car.

When I returned to my vehicle, the woman was standing at the trunk of my car calling a tow truck to have my car towed away. I stood there talking to the woman, trying to get her to move, so I could leave. Meanwhile, Princess and Gregory got out of the car and went to stand in the front of the car.

When I saw them, I went over to them, asking how they get out of the car and specifically how Gregory was able get out of his seatbelt that was across his booster seat. Princess said Gregory got out the car, and she followed him. I told him to show me how he got out of his booster seat. I put him back in the seat, and he wriggled his way out of the seatbelt without even unbuckling it. That was surprising.

Meanwhile, a tow truck pulled up along with a police officer. Fearing trouble, I called my husband, but he was at work. I called my grandmother, but she had no car. Upstairs, in one of the school's windows, the client who had told me about the school was watching the entire incident. She made her way down to us, walking directly over to me and the officer. The officer immediately stopped her saying, "Don't walk over here like that," halting her steps.

He began to question what I was doing, asking where I lived, and why I had left my children in the car. I explained to him that I was going over to the school to get a brochure. He proceeded to hurl insults at me, telling me I was probably not actually married and neither was I a resident of Rancho Cucamonga. Then, he began to ask what would be the point of getting information about school when I didn't even have a babysitter to watch them while I went to get the information.

Eventually, I pulled out my license, demonstrating I did actually live in Rancho Cucamonga and that I was indeed married. He said, "Oh well. You'll be getting arrested today, and you won't be able to come over here anymore." Then, the officer proceeded to tell me if I did not have anyone to pick up my children in twenty minutes, Child Protective Services would be called. My client prepared to drive my children to my grandmother's house. Throughout the entire incident, I was dumbfounded by the officer's words and actions. But what he did next, I was very unprepared for. He radioed for another officer, a black officer, to come to the scene to perform the arrest. Supposedly, my children would be permitted to leave, so they would not see me arrested. However, as my client began to drive away, the black officer placed the handcuffs on me, which my children did witness.

So, on that Friday, I was taken to jail. For the six days that I was there, I was unable to hold any food down, as I continued to regurgitate it. Over those days, I lost weight. While inside, awaiting a court date, I was told by the inmates and the public defender to not fight the case. Fighting the case would only cause me to stay inside longer. On the other hand, if I pled guilty, I would be permitted to go home. I was offered video court, but I refused because I wanted to appear before a live judge. Therefore, I had to wait until Tuesday or Wednesday before I was able to go.

When I stood before the judge, she offered me good luck with my career decision, and she apologized for the incident. During her discourse with me, I explained to her how I was told to plead. The only thing she could say was that she could not render any legal advice to me. In retrospect, I believe she was telling me to plead 'no contest.' However, in the moment, I pled guilty, as I had been instructed by others, because I desperately want to go home. The original charge was "willful cruelty to child/death," which is considered a felony. However, the charge was reduced to "willful cruelty to child," which is a misdemeanor. To say the least, I was happy to go home and see my family. That was the longest time I had been away from my children.

Up to that moment, I had heard an abundance of accounts from different people about their encounters with the police. Most of them were my clients, and as I stood braiding their hair, they would tell me about their experiences. All the time though, I was just an outsider looking into their situations based only on what I had heard. The encounter I had was my first negative experience with the police, and because of it, I finally understood what I had heard about time and time again. I must say, my personal experience caused me to look at police officers differently.

While still living in Alta Loma, I received an unexpected call from Princess' grandmother. She wanted to know if I would allow Princess' brother, who is Princess' same age, and her little sister, who is the same age as my son Jacob, to come live with me and my family for a while. She was asking because their mother had been arrested for registering a car her boyfriend (the father of her two children and Princess) had stolen. I am not sure if she was aware that car was stolen or not. What I do know is she paid the consequences for having it in her possession and attempting to claim it as her own. The children were unable to live with their father because he was already in jail, serving a five-year sentence.

After receiving the phone call, I spoke with my husband about it, we agreed to take the children in. So, for the next three months, we had five children in our home. Three months later, the children's mother was released from jail, and I returned her children to her when she and their grandmother came to pick them up. During that visit, she thanked me. And although she was grateful that I had cared for her children in her absence, she was not particularly happy the children's grandmother had not kept them with her. That had been her original request. She didn't care for me because of her feelings for Logan. His mother had them set up nicely, and I guess they were happy until it was found out that I was pregnant.

The grandmother, however, thought it would be better if someone who was younger and more energetic cared for them. Either way, I was happy to do it because I love children, and it gave Princess an opportunity to spend time with her brother and sister and get to know them better. From there, the children's mother and I developed somewhat of a relationship, seeing that my oldest child and her two children shared a father.

As the months passed by, I continued working with the lawyer to build a case against the hospital. On one particular day, Shonna's mother and I had to go through mediation with my lawyer and the hospital and its lawyer. During the mediation, the hospital tried very hard to paint a negative picture of Shonna by bringing up her past, including the time she went to jail, her past drug abuse, etc. The hospital's lawyer even went as far as to ask me if I knew about her heart disease and her history with drug abuse. I told them, "Regardless of all of that, she's not here today." I told them she had kept her doctor's appointments and she did what she was instructed as far as her pregnancy was concerned.

Throughout the entire mediation process, I was having contractions, and they were growing stronger and stronger as time went on. After a while, we decided to take a break. During that break, I told the hospital administration that I wanted to share something with them off the record. I explained to them that I had gone to their hospital myself recently because I had been suffering from dehydration. During that hospital visit, I was told to not get off the bed by myself, and if I required assistance, I was to press the nurse's call button.

While I was on the bed, a nurse came in to administer an IV bag. To do so, she had to move the table, on which the call button was placed, away from the bed. Once she finished administering the IV, she did not move the table back so the call button could be within my reach. Sometime later, I needed to go to the bathroom. But following their orders, I could not go to the bathroom alone. I looked for the button and saw that it was out of my reach. I had to lay there on the bed, unable to relieve myself, through excruciating pain. As I lay there, I wondered if that had happened to Shonna also.

I told them the reason I was sharing my experience with them was because it led me to wonder where Shonna's call button was. Was it in reach where she could have summoned a nurse when she found herself in trouble? I also informed them that I was insulted when they told me she had choked to death only to find out that was a complete lie. After the break, we resumed the mediation on record. The lawyers knew that my lawyer could use my personal experience against the hospital in Shonna's case, and I am sure they did not feel too good about that. A few more questions were asked of me and an apology was given for providing false information. Finally, the lawyers decided on an adjournment, not wanting me to go into labor at that time. Afterwards, I drove Shonna's mother back home all while still having contractions.

A couple of days later, I noticed a very large pimple on my thigh, and it was only getting bigger. It was bothering me, so I began to squeeze it, causing it to burst and the fluid inside to spill out. After the substance exuded from the pimple, burgundy veins were going up and down my legs. Eventually, it was hard to move one of my legs.

I decided I needed to go to the hospital to get my leg checked out. One of my younger brothers was at my house and decide to ride with me. I drove with one leg frozen in place, while my husband stayed home with the children. At the hospital, when I tell them what my problem was, they assessed me and told me I was in full labor. My cousin went by my house and picked up Isaac to bring him to the hospital. Upon her arrival, she took my brother back home with her. I found out there was an infection in my leg, and I would need antibiotics to clear the infection. However, I was required to deliver the baby first before I could ingest antibiotics. So, with one leg in a sling, I prepared to deliver my baby.

When my obstetrician checked my progress, he said I still had a little more to go to be fully dilated. He needed to go back to his clinic, so he told me he would be back soon. While he was gone, he left one of his residents to check on me. Before the resident checked my condition, he obtained my verbal permission. I told him it was fine with me.

Suddenly, I felt the urge to push. The obstetrician was called, letting him know I was ready to deliver, and he told them to tell me to wait. He turned around on his drive and began to make his way back to the hospital. While he was making his return, the pain I was experiencing was elevating, and my baby's heart rate was failing.

It was time to move forward with the delivery, without the obstetrician being there. So, the resident looked at me and asked me if he had permission to deliver my baby. I told him absolutely. So, on December 2, 2002, my daughter Ashonna was born. She was named after both Isaac's sister and my little sister, who have the middle name Ashonna, and to honor my stepmother Shonna who took me in and allowed me to live in her home with my other siblings. To her, I will always be grateful.

After my daughter was born, I was able to take the antibiotics to get rid of the infection that was in my leg. However, the antibiotics prevented me from breastfeeding my child, so she had to be bottle fed. Before leaving the hospital, I received flowers and a card from the resident, thanking me for allowing him to deliver my baby. My obstetrician also thanked me for allowing the resident to fill in. I said to him, "Thank you, too!" I understood how the resident felt. If I were in his position, I would have wanted someone to afford me the trust to attend to their medical needs, as I had plans to be in the medical field one day.

Upon leaving the hospital, I was determined to not get pregnant again. I tried different birth control methods, from the IUD to the NuvaRing and probably everything in between. However, I still got pregnant three more times. And each time, my obstetrician performed a DNC. I wanted my tubes to be tied, but my husband had to be in agreement. Finally, just over a year later in March 2004, my tubes were tied.

Let's step back a minute to 2003. When the year began, everything was **not** going normally. For one, after my beautiful baby daughter was born, an incident occurred that could have changed the course of our very lives. One day, I was home alone with her, as the other children were in preschool. She began to cry, and I did all I knew how to do. I gave her Tylenol; I gave her a bath; I fed her; and, I even gave her a massage. None of my efforts quelled the crying sounds that she emitted from her mouth. The crying seemed so loud to me, and it was literally driving me insane. My only other recourse was to pick up a pillow to smother the sounds.

Just as I lifted with the pillow to place over her face, something clicked inside my brain, saying, "Call your cousin." I placed the pillow back down on the couch, picked up my phone, and dialed my cousin's number. She wasted no time in coming over to my apartment. When she got there and saw my hysteria, she told me she would take my daughter off my hands. I was relieved and so grateful. My cousin kept Ashonna for the next week, giving me time to relax my mind and have some peace and quiet. I am grateful that the Holy Spirit stepped in and stopped my action that was more than likely caused from some type of postpartum depression.

Then in March, the second incident occurred. In an effort to improve my life and to tap into my desire for nursing, I began taking classes at Chaffee College. Up to that point, my husband and I had not experienced any serious problems (outside of the one with my sister). However, once I began to attend school, things changed. I began to see his insecurities with me going out of the house and into the world at large. Up to that point, he was the one who always took care of the business outside of the house, such as grocery shopping and taking care of other business. I usually stayed in the house, braiding hair sixteen to twenty hours a day and not really venturing out. Just as I had been when I was young, I was still a loner. That personality trait had obviously impacted the routine of our relationship. But unwelcomingly to Isaac, things were changing.

In the midst of dealing with his uncertainties regarding the changes that were taken place in my world, my husband decided to follow me to school one day. We only had one vehicle, a van, and I drove it to school. He had tried to convince me to stay home that day because it was the day after I had my tubes tied. However, I was adamant about going because I did not want to fall behind in my classes.

He was supposed to be home with the children, but instead, he left them alone to see if I was actually engrossed in school or if another man had my attention. The entire time he was on campus, I had no idea he was there. It wasn't until I returned home that I knew something was amiss. When I walked in the door, the apartment was a mess! The children were alone, and food was everywhere- all over the walls, etc. They had grown hungry and had tried to prepare themselves something to eat.

A few minutes later, Isaac walked through the door, telling me what he had done and how he hid in the back of the van and rode back to the house with me. He also told me he had no way of knowing if I ever cheated on him because I could no longer get pregnant. His words were alarming to me. And quite frankly, they made me feel creepy. Trying to calm his nerves, I explained to him that I had other desires than braiding. I wanted to be a nurse, and I needed to take classes for that to happen. It was nothing more and nothing less.

Despite my husband's discomforts, I enjoyed school, and it suited me well. Not only was it an outlet from being home all day with my children and braiding, but it was an opportunity to explore my other strengths. For example, while taking an English class, I was required to write different types of essays. On one of the essays, my professor wrote several positive comments, including one about my use of description. She also told me that I should consider going into writing. Her words warmed my heart. Through it all, I finished that semester and the one that followed.

After that, life returned to normal, and the fun moments were not too far away. That same month, it was time for another birthday celebration. One of my young cousins was turning thirteen, so my grandmother and I went into party planning mode. We decided to have the party in my apartment (even though by that time my grandmother and two young cousins had moved to the complex also), and we charged $2 per person. All the money went to the birthday girl.

The place was packed from wall to wall with friends and family, who were all laughing, eating, dancing, and having a great time. After that day, my already popular cousin became more popular with her school friends. That, of course, made her happy.

Within the few years of living in Alta Loma, my mother would come stay ever so often. We enjoyed our days of her being there. However, she wouldn't stay any more than three days. She would sleep and eat during most of her stay, and her nights often awakened me. She would shiver, shake, and sometimes yell my sister's name that had passed away. She would usually go back to Pomona when things got to that point.

On one particular night, she prayed with me before we went to bed. We were having a big court date the next day for the malpractice lawsuit. That was our first time praying together, except when we prayed over our food. She told me everything would be just fine because she could feel it.

The next day Jacob Jr, Dexter, and I arrived at court. We were joined by Pastor Nathan and his father Bishop Smith. We gathered and prayed before the hearing. After prayer, Dexter, who was only about two at the time, and I sat on a bench outside the courtroom. A woman walked over to us and complimented Dexter's dimples. He smiled and laughed. She asked if I was his mom, and I replied no. She then asked Dexter, "Where is your mom, handsome?" Dexter stood up on the bench and pointed his finger at the window toward the sky. I made eye contact with Jacob Jr, and we both had tears in our eyes. Dexter said, "Her up there."

I explained to the lady that Shonna had passed away, and the woman got teary eyed as well. That moment let us know Shonna was with us.

Court didn't take long at all. The judge decided in our favor. We calmly praised in the moment. After court, the lawyer told me I did a good job and explained how she would be splitting up the money between my siblings. I was relieved at the thought of less financial stress for my younger siblings when they became adults. My siblings who were already adults would receive their money right before my little sister Perris graduated high school. My younger siblings would receive theirs as each one turned eighteen, with interest from a trust fund account.

One day in August, my younger sister Perris and I were driving along when she looked over to me and said, "I think I might be pregnant." Dumbfounded, I looked over to her and said, "I didn't know you weren't a virgin." Then, I asked her who she lost her virginity to and she told me. Then, I asked her whom she was pregnant by, and she answered that question also. We drove to Walmart, got a pregnancy test, and went home to take the test. The test came back positive. Immediately, I asked her if she wanted to keep the baby. She said yes. At that point, I began giving her advice on what to do to prepare for her baby, telling her to make sure she keeps all her doctor's appointments.

She took my advice, and for the next nine months, she prepared to become a mother. For me, my house was becoming cramped with two adults and four children, so we moved from the two-bedroom apartment to a three bedroom in the same complex. That gave us a chance to spread out and breathe.

On the day Perris was scheduled to have her labor induced, I spent the entire day with her, taking her out to eat and to the movies. Then, I drove her to the hospital. When she had asked me to be with her during the delivery, I asked her if the father of the baby would be there, and she said yes. I told her that was great and to just let him be there with her. She insisted that I come along. She also requested for her godmother and her godfather to be there as well. On that day in April 2004, I became the proud aunt of a baby girl named Mariah.

Sometime near the end of the year, tragedy struck our family again. My niece's father, who was residing in Lancaster at the time, was shot in his head and killed. Perris and I, along with all of our siblings, went to the funeral service. At the end of the service, my sister came up to me and hugged me tightly. In my ear, she apologized for everything that she had done to me. She stated she had held animosity towards me because until I came into the picture, she had been the only girl. When I showed up on the scene, it took some of the attention away from her, and she felt as though I had taken her family away.

I told her it was all okay and that I was just trying to be her big sister. Her apology helped me to understand why certain things had occurred between us. At the same time though, it told me to be on the lookout for things that could occur in the future and to not be surprised if and when they did. So, from that point forward, I always used the mantra, "I'll love her with a long-handled spoon."

CHAPTER EIGHT
Out of Sight, Out of Mind

In 2005, Isaac was ready to leave California and move back to Vegas. Work for him was unstable, and he was tired of struggling. He had been asking me for quite a while to move the family back there. For me, California was a better fit because I had my braiding clients, and we had our own three-bedroom apartment, with low rent. If we were to move to Vegas, we would need to start from scratch. Meaning, we would both need to find jobs and a place to live.

After discussing our options at length, Isaac decided to make the move to Vegas, while I remained in California with the four children. He moved in with his mother and became employed by a local trash company. The company required him to work eight months, which would serve as a probation period, before he could become permanent.

Meanwhile, life in California remained the same, but progressively, things changed. For example, my oldest son Gregory began playing basketball, finding he really loved the game. He really had a love for *all* sports, even golf. He would take a plastic cup, a small ball, and a paper towel dowel and pretend to play golf in the kitchen. Then, he discovered his love for dressing up. On Sundays, he would wear suits and Stacey Adams to church. He loved his Stacey's so much that he would where them to school and even when he played basketball. I found his love for style simply adorable.

All of my children were making friends with the other children in the apartment complex. From time to time, some of those children would come to our home when their mother was cleaning her apartment. The break gave her peace of mind. When they were over, I braided, and they would play games and watch television.

As my children found their favorite pastimes, I was finding mine as well. One of my cousins decided to give me a makeover one day, by doing my nails and eyebrows (which was painful). I really liked how I looked and decided to keep the look going by getting my nails done often. Once again, I started wearing dresses and heels to church. From there, I went to a club with a young woman from the apartments, who lived next door to my grandmother. I had never gone to an adult club before, and I had a blast. After going a few more times, I was hooked, and clubbing became part of my life. At one point, I was going out on a regular basis, and the club life was wearing me out, making it hard for me to braid and go to work. I would find myself exhausted on a daily basis.

By then, I had begun working at Park West Hospital as a housekeeper, just to be in the medical environment and to add income to my household. While I was there, I ran into a family friend that I had known for some time. She was the girlfriend of the brother of a guy friend of mine. When she saw me, she said, "Alex was shot." From there, she told me which room he was in, and from that date forward, I would go into his room and pray with him. Thank God, he made it out of the hospital and is alive and well today.

My time working at the hospital would be short-lived though. I only worked from June to August because I lost my babysitter, who was my fourteen-year-old cousin who lived with my grandmother. She decided she could no longer babysit after my youngest son Jacob decided to walk out of the apartment one evening and cross the street to the Mobile Gas station. While he was there, a man saw him and was concerned because he was alone at two or three years old. The man bought Jacob a bag of potato chips and a soda. Another one of my cousins saw Jacob there, but not before the police were called.

Once Jacob was back home safely, the police called me from my house telling me to get home at once and that they were preparing to arrest my cousin. Their words scared the life from my cousin. In the end though, my cousin was not arrested, but it was recommended to me to have an older person care for my four children in my absence.

After that day, my cousin refused to babysit because she was concerned that something else would occur on her watch, and she did not want to be held liable. I understood her position, and I had to quit my job.

So, I know you are wondering how Jacob ended up at the gas station. Well, one day not too long before that, I was teaching Princess and Gregory how to cross the street, and obviously Jacob was paying attention. The morning my cousin babysat, she was upstairs in the townhouse, getting the kids dressed for the day. Meanwhile, Jacob was downstairs, and he opened the door, walked outside, and crossed the street to the store. So, my next conversation with him was to tell him to *not* do it again.

Meanwhile, Isaac and I would visit each other, by driving back and forth from California to Vegas and vice versa. Sometimes, he would show up in California unexpectedly, which was fine with me. Sometimes, I would not be home because I was out at the club. After missing some of his visits, I began to wean off the club scene. I got the sense that he thought I was cheating on him, and he wanted to catch me in the act. Other times, he would show up and not tell me at all that he had come by the apartment. The only way I knew he had been there was due to items being moved about, not being in the same place as I had left them. On other occasions, he would tell me he had come by and that I had not been home.

July rolled around, and it was party time again. My cousin Daisy was turning sixteen, so we planned a "Sweet Sixteen" party. And as usual, the party was at my apartment and included a $2 cover charge, which totaled about $300. Daisy was happy to get that chunk of change. She did give me $50 of it to have the carpet cleaned. Prior to the event, we prewarned the neighbors as a courtesy about the expected elevated noise level. They were fine with everything, and all went as planned:

great music, delicious food, and good company, until- a fight broke out. Two guys got into an altercation, and one pulled out a bat. The other guy took the bat from him and beat him with his own bat. How sad! Eventually, the police were called to break the fight up. That ended the party on a bad note, but despite that, everyone enjoyed themselves and was looking forward to the next event.

During that time, Princess's father was still in jail, serving his five-year sentence. He had found a way to make extra money by helping people make phone calls. Basically, he would call me, and I would make the call to the desired number for the inmates. I was the go-between. The inmates paid him for the calls, and he made sure my phone bill was paid by somehow filing taxes and having the refund sent to me. My phone bill was about $700, but the refund check covered it.

Shortly after that, I received an unexpected call. Isaac's brother-in-law called from Vegas and told me Isaac was cheating on me. I didn't know what to make of his phone call, but after thinking it over, I decided I did not believe he was telling me the truth for two reasons. First, there was an issue going on between Isaac's sister and his brother-in-law, and Isaac had become involved. So, I believed his brother-in-law was calling me as retaliation for Isaac getting involved in his marital affairs. Second, Isaac had been coming to see me, and I was going to see him. We had been working on building our relationship. I decided not to mention the phone call to Isaac. I just kept it to myself and continued having faith that my husband was not cheating on me.

As the year came to a close, in November 2005, Isaac had become permanent on his job and had rented an apartment. So, I decided it was time for me and our children to move to Vegas. During the same time, my sister and Jacob Jr. had gotten into a heated disagreement, and she needed to move out on her own for the very first time. After she and I talked things over, it was decided she would take over my three-bedroom apartment, using her own income to qualify. When the apartment manager agreed, Perris moved in, and I moved out.

Moving to Vegas, I left California in my rearview mirror. I was happy to not have to work as much. Instead, I was free to braid and go back to school. I began taking classes at CSN, and several of my California clients would carpool to Vegas to get their hair braided, and I gained more clients who lived in Vegas.

Back in California, Perris was wreaking havoc at the apartment building. She would go into the office, with an irate attitude, making comments about her rent, thinking she was being charged from my income as well. I called and assured her that it was her apartment, based on her income, and that my name was no longer on the lease.

I was receiving calls about the aroma of marijuana emitting from her apartment and there being too many people inside. Finally, the apartment manager said Perris had incurred too many violations and she had to go. I completely understood. Perris was given an opportunity to have peace and quiet in her own apartment, with just herself and her daughter, but she blew it. She had to face the consequences. There was nothing I could do to prevent the actions of the manager.

2006 started off great. Between my braiding and course schedules and Isaac's work schedule, we found time to have date nights here and there. Thankfully, his sister babysat for us, giving us a chance to go out and be alone. During that time, we were happy, and our life felt as it should have felt long ago. We were financially stable. I was finally less stressed. I was able to braid because I wanted to not because I had to. Isaac was able to provide, so he was feeling confident.

When February came around, Isaac took me out for my birthday. He took me shopping, we ate at a high-end restaurant, we played a few slot machines, and we watched a beautiful water show at the Bellagio Hotel that brought tears to my eyes. Overall, we had a great time. I was excited that things were great and was ecstatic and motivated about moving forward and progressing in our futures.

Ten days later, while sitting on the couch watching a movie together, his sister called, and I handed him the phone. I continued to watch the movie until I heard his tone of voice change. I turned to look at him, and he was red in the face. He said, "I'll be down there in a minute." He stood from the couch and while walking down the hall, he punched the wall making a dent. Then, he walked out the door.

To be continued in Volume II.

www.ingramcontent.com/pod-product-compliance
Lightning Source LLC
Chambersburg PA
CBHW072009090426
42734CB00033B/2321